Marriage

OWNER'S MANUAL

Marriage

OWNER'S MANUAL

Linda Hertel Dykstra, Ph.D.

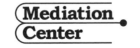

of Grand Rapids, Michigan

Book design by The Last Word; Grand Rapids, MI
Editorial assistance by James Vanden Bosch; Calvin College, Grand Rapids, MI
Cover design by Green Parrot Graphics/John Plummer; Grand Rapids, MI
Printed by Color House Graphics; Grand Rapids, MI

LIBRARY OF CONGRESS CATALOGING–IN–PUBLICATION DATA

Hertel Dykstra, Linda.
    Marriage Owner's Manual/ Linda Hertel Dykstra.
    p. cm.
    Includes Bibliographical references.
    ISBN 0-9665503-0-7
    1. Marriage--Psychological aspects. 2. Interpersonal relations.
      3. Divorce Mediation.
    I. Title.
HQ734.H537 1996
306.81--dc20   96-28825
                                                            CIP

COPYRIGHT ©1997, 1998 BY LINDA HERTEL DYKSTRA, PH.D.
                  SECOND EDITION PUBLISHED BY
                  MEDIATION CENTER OF GRAND RAPIDS
                  2716 EAST PARIS, SE
                  GRAND RAPIDS, MI 49546
                  PREVIOUSLY PUBLISHED BY
                  NOVA SCIENCE PUBLISHERS, INC.
                  COMMACK, NEW YORK , 1997.

The author and publisher have taken care in preparation of this book but make no expressed or implied warranty of any kind and assume no responsibility for any errors or omissions. No liability is assumed for incidental or consequential damages in connection with or arising out of information contained in this book.

This publication is designed to provide accurate and authoritative information with regard to the subject matter covered herein. It is sold with the clear understanding that the publisher is not engaged in rendering legal or any other professional services. If legal or any other expert assistance is required, the services of a competent person should be sought. FROM A DECLARATION OF PARTICIPANTS JOINTLY ADOPTED BY A COMMITTEE OF THE AMERICAN BAR ASSOCIATION AND A COMMITTEE OF PUBLISHERS.

Printed in the United States of America

DEDICATION

This book is dedicated to the three most supportive people in my life: my mother, father, and husband. Each of them has unconditionally loved me and consistently encouraged me to self-actualize. My parents' sixty-year marriage and my own three-decade relationship verify that intimate, enduring marriages are possible. This book is written so that others may experience the joy of a long-term relationship.

Contents

DESIGN

OPERATION

REPAIR

BREAKDOWN

REBUILDING

LIST OF DIAGRAMS
AND CHARTS

DESIGN

OPERATION

REPAIR

CHAPTER 9: OPTIONS SHORT OF DIVORCE

BREAKDOWN

CHAPTER 10: TRADITIONAL PROCESS
VERSUS DIVORCE MEDIATION

REBUILDING

CHAPTER 11: TASKS OF ADJUSTMENT

ACKNOWLEDGMENTS

From the moment I entered the practice of psychology, this book was destined to be written. It is the culmination of many years of training and experience: my training as both a psychologist and a mediator, the clinical hours I have spent with clients, and various other professional experiences. At this point, it is difficult to know whom to credit for each of the specific concepts described in this book.

However, my deep appreciation is extended to the authors and theorists who have most directly affected my professional orientation: Eric Erickson, Carl Rogers, Robert Carkhuff, Bernard Berenson, Alfred Adler, Bernard Kaplan, Aaron Beck, William Ury, and Roger Fisher. In addition, I wish to thank my clients. Through their growth, they have taught me much of what is now presented here. It is my belief that the principles which assisted them can benefit others as well.

A special word of thanks is also extended to several of my colleagues: psychologists Hap Frizzel, Kirk Brink, and Mary DeYoung, and attorneys John Grostic and James Howard. They, along with my dear husband, have motivated, inspired, and encouraged me in this endeavor.

Last, I express my sincere appreciation to those who directly assisted with the manuscript. John Grostic and Leona Hertel critiqued the initial version. James Vanden Bosch, professor of English at Calvin College, made the final editorial revisions. Cynthia Hooper and the staff at The Last Word did all of the word-processing related to the manuscript. Their help has been invaluable.

Marriage OWNER'S MANUAL is based on my clinical work rather than research. It is a self-help book rather than an academic treatise. Accordingly, the bibliography includes a variety of vintage titles which have proven helpful to both the author and her clients as they have worked with the concepts and skills discussed herein. Various categories–values, assertiveness, dysfunctional family including incest, forgiveness, mediation, grief, divorce, children and divorce–are listed, with several titles cited in each category.

For clarity and simplicity, this book is similar in format to that of a car owner's manual. It is divided into five major sections: Design, Operation, Repair, Breakdown, and Rebuilding. It covers all phases of a relationship.

Design: If the relationship is just beginning, the book can be used to teach the reader the criteria and skills necessary to select a mate and make a marriage work.

Operation: If the relationship is well established and vigorous, the manual can be used to clarify why it is strong.

Repair: If the relationship is struggling, *Marriage OWNER'S MANUAL* can be used to diagnose where the relationship falls short and what needs to be done to improve the situation.

Breakdown: If the relationship is beyond repair, the book can be used to help the reader choose between the traditional divorce process and the creative option of divorce mediation.

Rebuilding: If divorce has already occurred, the manual can help the reader understand why the marriage ended and how to design a new and successful relationship in the future.

Just as an automobile owner's manual is a resource which accompanies a new car, *Marriage OWNER'S MANUAL* is a guidebook for a human relationship.

DESIGN

CHAPTER 1

VALUES

Washington, D.C., comes alive in the spring. Tourists multiply and merge in a kaleidoscope of shapes and colors. They move from monument to museum with maps in hand and children in tow. Street vendors sell spicy hot dogs and a potpourri of souvenirs. The cherry trees burgeon with blossoms. Brightly clothed joggers weave up and down the mall, while paddle boats bob in the reflecting pool of the nearby Jefferson Memorial.

Two young bicyclists blend into this bustling scene. As they pedal past the Capitol Building, Betsy shouts over her shoulder to Tricia, "How about a break? Let's stop at the ice cream parlor and get a double dip in a waffle cone."

"Sounds great. Let's order the usual, black cherry for you and tin roof for me," Tricia responded.

"Right," said Betsy as she stopped, set her kick stand, and started toward the window to place their order. Simultaneously, Tricia reserved two wrought-iron chairs. She dropped into one and put her helmet on the other. She and Betsy, who were roommates at the University of Maryland, had perfected this routine.

Betsy returned with their ice cream cones. They licked, dripped, laughed, and talked. "When I called my grandparents today, they invited us to come down to visit them in Ft. Lauderdale over Easter vacation. What do you think of that idea? Are you interested?"

Without waiting for an answer, she went on. "It might be time for a real spring break. This could be our last opportunity. Who knows what next year will bring? We both might be involved in job hunting and interviews."

"Hmm. Florida." Betsy considered the idea as she nibbled her ice cream cone. "We would want action and a place to stay."

"My grandparents have an extra bedroom. Their place is near the Ft. Lauderdale beach and boardwalk." She swung her head in cadence as she spoke. "Tunes and tanning, rhythm and romance."

Betsy laughed. "The more you talk, the better it sounds. When we get back to the sorority, let's call your grandparents and confirm the offer. I think my parents would be open to the idea. They don't expect me to come home. In fact, they plan to be away during Easter vacation."

Since both of Betsy's parents were educators, they were free to travel over spring break. Her mother was an elementary school teacher in Landover, Maryland, where the family lived. Her father was a professor at a nearby junior college. Both parents enjoyed not only the nature of their profession, but also the balance of their work and leisure time. They particularly appreciated having their summers free.

Each season, they kept their vintage sailboat at Annapolis, near the United States Naval Academy. The family spent summer weekends on the boat. It had become a way of life which provided relaxation and togetherness. The Chesapeake Bay was beautiful and, with the Academy nearby, Betsy always enjoyed an active social life.

Her parents were involved in their large Catholic Church, which was active in the local community and had an outreach ministry in the inner city. They thoroughly appreciated the greater Washington, D.C., area. Betsy felt at home on the East Coast and wished to eventually find a teaching position in the vicinity.

In contrast to the rather laid-back lifestyle of Betsy's mother and father, Tricia's parents were hard driving and career oriented. Her mother was an attorney, and her father was a stockbroker and financial planner. In order to have easy access to their jobs in downtown Washington, D.C., they lived in Georgetown. They enjoyed the culture of the city and often attended events at the Kennedy Center and the National Theatre. They worshipped at the Washington National Cathedral, where they enjoyed both the beauty of the edifice and the formality of the service.

Betsy, a petite blonde with a mischievous grin and quick laugh, and Tricia, a tall brunette with a fun-loving personality, were placed together in college housing during their first year. They became close friends and remained roommates. Both were free spirits who shared a sense of humor. They were adventuresome and bright. Their fellow students at the university called them the undaunted duo. The present idea about the Florida trip developed in their usual spontaneous manner.

As they traveled back to campus, they discussed the possibility further. They created the perfect rationale. It was their junior year, and who could guess where each of them would be next spring? It was their last opportunity before they found jobs in their chosen professions of education and accounting. Besides, except for gas and meals, the trip would be free.

That evening Tricia phoned her grandparents and reconfirmed their offer. They were eager to have the two young women visit over spring break. Then she called home. As expected, she easily attained parental consent.

It was Betsy's turn. She phoned her parents. After they recorded the name and telephone number of Tricia's grandparents, along with the dates of the trip, they also approved. The two coeds were set to go. Betsy's sub-compact car would provide the necessary transportation, although it would be a challenge to pack all of the desired items–suitcases, sun chairs, towels, beach balls, and tote bags.

At about the same time but many miles away, a similar vacation idea germinated at the University of Wisconsin when Ben and Tom took a study break. "This anatomy and physiology course is really tough. I feel like a zombie. I'm glad Easter break is coming," Ben said with frustration in his voice.

In response, his friend Tom enthusiastically began singing strains of "Happy Days Are Here Again." As he built to a crescendo, he made an expansive gesture with his arms. He concluded the song at maximum volume. Fortunately, they were alone in the study room of their fraternity. Ben laughed and cheered for an encore.

With this encouragement, Tom vigorously tapped his hands on the table as he spoke. "Just one more week until freedom. It's time to cut loose and let the good times roll. Wouldn't a vacation, you know, a real vacation, be great? Shall we rock-climb in Yellowstone, ski in Colorado, or do something a little more awesome like looking cool and collegiate in Florida?" Without a pause for a response, he continued. "I vote for Florida. We are such serious dudes. Let's change our style and attitude for one full week."

Ben stopped short and deliberated. He spoke slowly. "Actually, we might be able to pull off a Florida trip. Dave and Dick are going south with Carl when he goes home to Ft. Lauderdale for spring break. At lunch, Carl gave an open invitation to everyone at the table to join the three of them. His parents have a couple of spare rooms now that their children are grown. According to Carl, his parents said they'd love to have as many of us as wished to come. 'The more the merrier,' to quote Carl. What do you think?"

Ben and Tom were roommates by choice. The two young men had been friends since they started kindergarten. They grew up in Oshkosh, where Ben's mother was a licensed practical nurse who worked at the nearby hospital. She opted to work the longer shifts so she could have extended, uninterrupted time at home with the family. She enjoyed being a homemaker. His father sold and serviced farm equipment.

His family was involved in their small Baptist Church. They expressed their Christian love not only in the worship service, but also in their concern for others, concern exhibited on a daily basis. As Ben grew up, he heard about dealing with people in the medical setting as well as in the sales and service business. He himself planned to be a physical therapist.

Ben was tall and slender. He had a warm smile and a gentle disposition. Although he genuinely liked people, he was quiet and unobtrusive. In contrast, Tom was an extrovert.

Tom's parents owned a large dairy farm which had belonged to his paternal grandparents. He appreciated growing up there even though it was hard work. His family was very committed to the Assemblies of God Church. Their religion embodied their sense of connectedness to the Lord, each other, and the land.

Early on, Tom decided to become a veterinarian and have a large-animal practice. He liked how Doc Art had cared for his parents' herd over the years, and he wanted to be the same kind of doctor and do the same quality work.

Often, in order to earn both spending money and his college tuition, Ben worked with Tom on the farm. Being together long hours enhanced their friendship. They were like brothers. When they went to college, they made certain they were roommates. They shared a common history and a comfortable relationship filled with good humor.

Tom had a dark complexion. He was about the same height as Ben but more muscular. He made friends with anyone, anywhere, anytime. If he went to the service station where his pickup truck was being repaired, he hung over the engine with the mechanic and discussed spark plugs and crankshafts. When he traveled, he discussed politics with the man in the three-piece suit. He intuited the issues of greatest interest to his companion. Perhaps that is why he was so good with animals. He could sense their needs without the spoken word.

His personality propelled him to the office of Class Vice President during his third year and to Class President in his fourth. He was personable and bright. He already had been accepted into the Veterinary Medicine School at Michigan State University–he thought he should broaden his horizons and move out of state.

Both Ben and Tom were seniors. Next year they would be in their respective graduate programs and no longer be roommates and have the same academic calendar. Consequently, this was their last opportunity to share a spring vacation together.

Ben repeated his question, "What do you think? Shall we go to Florida and stay with Carl's family?"

Tom paused. "I'd need to check with my parents to make certain they don't need me on the farm...." His sentence drifted off. He sat silently. Suddenly his eyes brightened and his body became energized. "It could be my graduation gift. Awesome. I wonder if they would buy that idea. I'll call them and see." He leaped for the phone on the wall of the study room.

Ben listened as Tom talked with his parents. He was always so persuasive. When he hung up the phone, he had an expansive grin. "Yes. Let's make plans with Carl."

Ben reacted. "Just a minute. I still have to talk with my parents. Hit the road while I call them."

"OK. I'm out of here." Tom left the study room. When he returned a few minutes later, Ben was humming his favorite country and western song. His parents' answer was obvious. The two of them would pack the back of Tom's well-worn pickup truck, snap on the canvas cover, and be on their way next Friday. Carl's parents would be accommodating five college seniors.

The week seemed longer than usual, but Friday finally came. Both sets of roommates, Tricia and Betsy from Maryland and Tom and Ben from Wisconsin, packed their vehicles and headed to Florida. Since it was spring vacation on nearly every major university campus, the roads were filled with other young people driving south.

Both sets of roommates arrived Saturday evening. Tricia and Betsy settled into Tricia's grandparents' spacious guest bedroom, which overlooked a courtyard filled with tropical flowers. Tom and Ben made themselves comfortable in their room at Carl's parental home. It was obvious that this room had belonged to Carl's brothers, the twins. The bunk beds had brown bedspreads with horses woven into them. As they unpacked, Ben and Tom assumed a western drawl and called each other "pardner" in true John Wayne fashion. They twanged and chuckled.

Although the five young men were tired, they couldn't go to bed until they had checked out the boardwalk. The activity along the beach revived them. They walked, talked, and had a hamburger and fries before retiring for the evening.

In the morning, the Florida skies were gray and the air was filled with a light drizzle. Tricia and Betsy revised their plans. Instead of going to the beach, they headed for the shops on the boardwalk. Tom and Ben did likewise while Carl, Dick, and Dave drove to the Everglades.

Clothing stores, bathing suit shops, restaurants, pubs, and a huge T-shirt and novelty store made the morning interesting. Tricia and Betsy lingered in the T-shirt shop, which had a variety of shirts, including those that could be silk-screened to order.

They liked the idea of personalized shirts. As they generated whimsical options, they laughed gleefully. Finally, they made a decision and ordered two hot-pink T-shirts with a turtle motif. On the front was the smiling face of a terrapin. On the back were his jaunty legs and tail.

As the shirts were being completed, Betsy wondered aloud if anyone would realize that this happy terrapin was the University of Maryland mascot. As she mused, Tom and Ben entered the store.

With his usual efficiency, Tom quickly surveyed both the merchandise and the clientele. When he spotted Tricia and Betsy, he came over in his extroverted manner and pretended to be a clerk.

"May I help you, ladies? We have the highest quality T-shirts with only the catchiest slogans." Ben stood quietly at his elbow and smiled broadly.

Tricia and Betsy laughed warmly. Then Tricia responded in kind. "We have already placed our order, sir, but may we assist you in your selection?"

"Of course, madam," said Tom. The relationship among the four of them was off to a light-hearted start.

When their T-shirts were finished, Tricia and Betsy showed Tom and Ben. Immediately Tom stated, "You both must attend the University of Maryland." Tricia and Betsy were very impressed.

As they talked, Tricia was drawn to Tom's exuberance, and Betsy found Ben's quiet warmth very appealing. The foursome seemed perfect. The week was off to an exciting start. During the days that followed, they shared sunshine and sand, laughter and late nights. But the week was all too short.

As the exhilarating vacation wound to a close, both couples were reluctant to part. The trip had more than met their expectations, but now it was about to end.

As they discussed the upcoming separation, Tom had two ideas which he labeled as sterling. First, they should find a photo booth so that each of them could have a set of pictures as proof that their perfect week really had happened. This idea was unanimously supported.

Off they went to locate a photo booth. Although it was challenging, they succeeded. The four of them squeezed onto the tiny seat and pulled the curtain closed; they jostled, laughed, and posed as the camera flashed.

Afterwards, as they made their way to the hot dog stand for lunch, Tom shared the second sterling idea. As couples, they could separate later rather than sooner if Ben and Betsy drove together to the Florida state line in Betsy's car and Tricia and Tom traveled in his pickup truck. They could stay in tandem until they reached the border. The plan was heartily endorsed.

The next day, while riding together, each couple had opportunity for more serious conversation. Tricia talked about her life plan to become a CPA and eventually a partner in a large public accounting firm on the East coast. Tom shared his goal of being a veterinarian with a large-animal practice in the Midwest. They each spoke about their families, life experiences, and dreams for the future. Although there were significant differences, neither seemed to notice.

As they chatted, Tricia invited Tom to Washington, D.C., after graduation. Tricia wanted to show him the highlights of the city she loved and have him experience the environment in which she thrived. They agreed to write to establish the exact dates and specific plans.

Simultaneously, Betsy and Ben had a similar conversation. They too decided on a reunion. Ben planned to come to Washington, D.C., in mid-summer. He had never been to the nation's capital. Betsy was eager to be his tour guide.

The stage was set for both pairs to develop a relationship. As is already apparent, there are greater social, economic, and vocational differences between Tricia and Tom than between Betsy and Ben. If both couples pursue their respective relationships to the point of marriage, what are the long-term implications of these differences? That question will be considered in respect to the five components relevant to designing a successful relationship, beginning with the concept of values. Shared values are the first dimension to consider for an enduring relationship.

Values: Definition

Values are the principles or beliefs by which all of us, including Tricia, Tom, Betsy, and Ben, live our lives. Values are the core of our being, the essence of who we are. They are our deepest, most significant guiding principles and beliefs.

In light of what we know about Tricia, Betsy, Tom, and Ben in regard to the home, social, and religious environment in which each of them was raised, we can guess what some of their respective values might be. Tricia would value educational and professional success, money, material possessions, a high personal and professional profile, life in a major city on the East Coast, and continued involvement in the Episcopalian Church. Betsy would value education, adequate funds for a comfortable lifestyle, service to others, quality family time, and continued involvement in the Catholic Church, including outreach to those in need.

Tom's list might include the agrarian lifestyle, service to others, compassion and helpfulness to animals, cooperative and helpful human relationships, enough money to live comfortably, involvement in the Assemblies of God Church, and dependence on

God. Ben would appreciate education, medicine, service to others, involvement in the Baptist Church, and love for God and others.

Let's leave Tricia, Betsy, Tom, and Ben for a time and move to a broader discussion of the topic of values. As stated earlier, values are the principles or beliefs by which we live our lives. They are the core of our being, the essence of who we are. They are our deepest, most significant guiding principles and beliefs.

To illustrate, if you value honesty and believe that honesty is the best policy, you will try to live your life in as truthful a fashion as possible. You will be forthcoming even if there is a personal price to pay.

Let's say you have a used car for sale and it has a broken odometer. If you have inadvertently reported incorrect mileage to a potential buyer, you will correct the misinformation even if it means you may lose the sale. Your first and foremost goal is honesty.

Or consider another example. If you and your spouse share the belief that acceptance of others is a cardinal principle of life, you will seek to live your lives with tolerance. You will avoid criticism, gossip, and judgment. You will exercise acceptance.

If you are out to dinner with neighbors and they begin to denigrate mutual friends, you would interact as follows.

Husband:	"Can you believe John and Ruth bought that riding lawn mower when they have filed for bankruptcy?"
Wife:	"It certainly seems irresponsible to me. Of course, they would not need to declare bankruptcy if they were responsible."
You:	"There are two sides to every story. We don't know all of the facts. They may need to keep the lawn looking good in order to sell the house. They plan to move to a smaller one as soon as possible. They are trying to balance expenses with their income."

Your Spouse: "The riding mower may be a means to that end. They may be smarter than we think."

You have taken charge of the conversation, neutralized it, and reversed the outcome. You supported rather than criticized, thereby honoring your commitment to tolerance and acceptance.

VALUES: NON-NEGOTIABLE AND NEGOTIABLE

There are two major categories of values: non-negotiable and negotiable. Non-negotiable values are beliefs and principles on which you are inflexible, immovable, and unwilling to compromise. Non-negotiable values cannot comfortably be altered or negotiated. No matter what the circumstances or potential outcome, you must honor them.

The foregoing examples related to honesty and acceptance represent not only values but also non-negotiable values. Based on your own internal standards, you had no options other than the ones exercised.

In the example related to honesty, you had to correct the misinformation about the mileage if you were to be at peace with yourself. In the example related to acceptance, it was necessary to stop the criticism no matter what the personal price. To be true to your non-negotiable values is to be true to yourself and vice versa.

In the second category are negotiable values. Negotiable values are beliefs on which you are flexible and able to compromise. They are pliable and adaptable, and they can be molded to the situation or desired outcome.

With the same examples related to honesty and acceptance, let's imagine that the values are negotiable rather than non-negotiable. In both cases, you have options. In the first illustration, if it looked like correcting the mileage information might affect the sale, you could choose to either rectify or not rectify depending on how desirous you were to sell the car. Honesty would be negotiable.

In the second example, if your commitment to acceptance was negotiable and perhaps less important than the continuation of your friendship with your dinner partners, you might choose to gossip and criticize. The conversation might sound like this.

Husband: "Can you believe John and Ruth bought that riding lawn mower when they have filed for bankruptcy?"

Wife: "It certainly seems irresponsible to me. Of course, they would not need to declare bankruptcy if they were responsible."

You: "I was amazed too. They have always overspent, and that irresponsible behavior just does not stop. Think of what they teach their children. The mismanagement just goes on and on. Their children will probably follow in their footsteps."

Your Spouse: "What a mess."

Two further illustrations will demonstrate the differences between non-negotiable and negotiable values. Imagine that your definition of being a true friend includes being loyal and supportive through good times and bad. You are scheduled to leave on a camping trip. On the day of departure, your dear friend's father dies.

If your value of being a loyal and supportive friend is non-negotiable, you will postpone the trip, no matter how complicated postponement might be, so that you can be there during these difficult days. If it is negotiable, you will have various options. If it is easy to rearrange your departure for a day or two, you might do so. If it is complicated, you might simply call your friend, extend your condolences, send flowers, and leave on your trip.

A second example involves keeping promises. Imagine that you are a furniture salesperson. In addition to selling, you place the order and specify the delivery date. If keeping your promise is non-negotiable, you are responsible and state a realistic delivery date. Even if the sale might hinge on that date, you state the time at which you truly can produce the furniture. It is very important to you to make a promise you truly can keep.

If, on the other hand, honoring your word is negotiable, you could determine the date the customer desires and promise delivery by that time even if it might be impossible to do so. Although you cannot meet the date, you have made the sale. As the deadline approaches and passes, you create the necessary excuses.

Non-negotiable values cannot be comfortably altered and modified. In fact, if you negotiate them, you feel uncomfortable and disquieted. If you have a non-negotiable value about being a true friend but leave on your trip as planned, you have a guilty conscience. A guilty conscience causes the emotional discomfort you feel when your behavior lies outside of your non-negotiable values.

While you are away on your camping trip, your mind repeatedly returns to your friend's grief. Your vacation is less enjoyable because you not only think of your friend but also feel disappointed in yourself. You have let down your friend, but equally, if not more important, you have done the same to yourself. You struggle with a deep sense of personal disappointment because you have violated your own non-negotiable value.

If you have a non-negotiable value about promises and you let the furniture sale itself outweigh that value, it is difficult for you to live with yourself. Although you may have made the sale and can anticipate a handsome commission, you feel miserable when you know you cannot meet the deadline. You have not been true to yourself and have not honored your non-negotiable value about promises. You continue to think about the situation, feel disappointed in yourself, and experience a guilty conscience.

A guilty conscience alerts you to the fact that your present behavior lies outside of your non-negotiable values. What you are doing does not fit with what you believe.

If from time to time you experience disappointment and disquiet, look for the non-negotiable value that you are violating. Be aware that these feelings will not disappear until you bring your behavior back in line with your non-negotiable values.

In the situation related to being a true friend, in order to relieve your emotional discomfort, you could either call while you were on the trip or talk with your friend as soon as you arrived home and apologize for not being there when needed. Further, you could pledge not to negotiate this non-negotiable value in the future.

In the second situation, you could go to the customer and explain that you were unrealistic when you set the delivery date. Or, you could decide to live through this experience and determine to not make this mistake again. In the future, you would aim to consistently give a realistic delivery date even if it meant the loss of the sale.

The best way to truly know yourself is to know your own non-negotiable values. Your non-negotiable values are the core of who you are. They are the basis on which you make decisions. They create the road map you need to navigate through life with your personal integrity intact.

VALUES: DEVELOPMENT

When we think of the values discussed thus far–honesty, acceptance, friendship, keeping promises–how is it possible that for some people these values are non-negotiable and for others they are negotiable? The answer lies in our maturation process. Every person has a unique developmental experience. All of us grow up in different homes and attend different schools and churches. Our parents, teachers, and church leaders model a variety of values.

In addition to these variables, each child is a unique person. Thus, there is an interaction between what is taught and modeled by our parents, teachers, church leaders, and our own individuality. In terms of individuality, it is interesting to note that even though siblings grow up in the same home, they may not ultimately adopt identical non-negotiable values.

Values are taught and modeled primarily by parents. For example, if your mother and father live a self-disciplined life, this value is demonstrated to you. If your mother and father manage their time well and meet their deadlines at the job and at home, you see first-hand how an organized, responsible life works. If your mother and father believe that a personal relationship with God is important, they will not only tell you this but also will model it through personal and family devotional time, as well as by regular church attendance.

Although parents are the primary source of values while children grow up, the school and church are solid secondary sources. For example, if a teacher gives stickers for each book read, the values of reading and learning are reinforced. If your priest preaches about the forgiveness and compassion Joseph had for his brothers after they sold him into slavery (Genesis 45), or your minister has a sermon on the parable of the prodigal son and how his father forgave him and loved him in spite of his irresponsible life (Luke 15), the values of forgiveness and compassion are taught. When, in church school, each child is encouraged to bring a Christmas present for homeless children, the value of compassion is reinforced and the value of generosity is added.

As children move into adolescence, they begin to pick and choose from all of the values taught by their parents, school, and church. They select the ones they will hold as non-negotiable. One of the major developmental tasks of adolescence is value clarification.

Initially, teenagers may throw off most of the values modeled. Self-discipline, personal relationship with God, education, forgiveness, compassion, and generosity may be cast aside. Although this may seem like rebellion, it actually is the first step of the sorting process. After they discard, they begin to reassess and decide which they wish to keep. One by one, they begin to reclaim various values taught by their parents, school, and church.

For example, after association with a wild crowd, a teenager may begin to select friends who are self-disciplined, religious, academic, forgiving, compassionate, and generous. Further, these values may be demonstrated as the young person begins to tutor children who have academic problems or drive those without transportation to church. This same youth may begin to read books about Abraham

Lincoln or Eleanor Roosevelt, people who embody many of these principles. The values chosen and the behaviors exhibited are congruent.

It should be noted that by the time young people reach their late teens and early twenties, their non-negotiable beliefs are fairly well established. If you are that age or older, your values are stable. Who you are now is basically who you will be for the remainder of your life. Your core principles and values are established.

As teenagers become clearer about their non-negotiable values, they make decisions that mesh with these values. They choose friends based on these beliefs. It should be noted that friendships work best when non-negotiable values are shared. The more similar they are, the more compatible and conflict-free the relationship is likely to be.

The same is true in terms of spouses. The closer the match between you and your partner, the more compatible the relationship. Thus, the first component necessary to design an enduring marriage is a set of shared non-negotiable values.

So far, we have talked about the values of honesty, acceptance, friendship, keeping promises, self-discipline, relationship to God, reading and learning, forgiveness, compassion, and generosity. There are many others that you might cherish, such as trustworthiness, confidentiality, independence, autonomy, respect, persistence, goal-directedness, genuineness, sincerity, creativity, planning, organization, fairness, spontaneity, humor, warmth, love, responsibility, kindness, courtesy, tactfulness, optimism, and responsible money management. Any quality that is important to you can be a value.

Even though you have already gone through adolescence and have developed your value system, you may never have attempted to clarify and list your values for yourself. You may not have brought them to a conscious level in an organized way. Perhaps you have neither thought of your adolescence as a time of value clarification nor ever stopped to reflect on them and list them.

Most of us do not consider our lives within the framework of non-negotiable values. We simply make decisions because they seem right, and then move forward. We do not analyze which beliefs most directly affect which decisions. We use our road map more by intuition than by knowledge.

As you seek to more fully know yourself and understand the components necessary for an enduring relationship, it would be helpful to look more closely at your road map. It would be beneficial to clarify your values so that you can make decisions, including the selection of a spouse, as wisely as possible.

If you are already married, value clarification will help you better understand the nature of the similarities and differences between the two of you. If you experience repeated conflict in your relationship, it will be beneficial to identify the value differences which underlie this stress.

VALUE CLARIFICATION

To aid you in the process of your personal value clarification, think about your childhood. On page 24, record the values your parents taught and modeled. To help you complete the column labeled *Parents*, think of the values discussed in this chapter: honesty, acceptance, friendship, keeping promises, organization, self-discipline, personal relationship with God, education, forgiveness, compassion, and generosity.

Think of the others also mentioned, namely, trustworthiness, confidentiality, independence, autonomy, respect, persistence, goal-directedness, genuineness, sincerity, creativity, planning, organiza-tion, fairness, spontaneity, humor, warmth, love, responsibility, kindness, courtesy, tactfulness, optimism, and responsible money management. Further, consider the behaviors for which you were rewarded or disciplined.

In addition, recall the mottoes you heard when you were a child. Parents often use wise sayings to teach values. For example, "if you can't say anything nice, don't say anything at all." The two principles being taught are "think before you speak" and "be kind." Or, "success is ninety-nine percent perspiration and one percent inspiration," which emphasizes the necessity of hard work and persistence. Or again, "if it is worth doing, it is worth doing well," which encourages a commitment to excellence. A story will illustrate how values are taught.

One day a little girl walked home from elementary school. As she passed the old white frame house on the corner near her home, an elderly lady called out to her. "Little girl. Little girl. If I give you the money, will you go to the store and buy a loaf of bread for me?"

"Yes," said the child as she ran up the steps to get the money. The lady placed several coins in her hand. As the little girl left the house, she counted the money and found there was not enough for a loaf of bread. Perplexed, she ran home to tell her mother.

After she explained the situation, her mother praised her for her desire to help the elderly woman (compassion and empathy), and gave her the additional coins needed to make the purchase (sharing and generosity). Off went the child to buy the bread.

When she returned to the woman's house and handed her the loaf of bread, she did not tell the lady about the shortfall. Rather, she smiled proudly. As she skipped home, she had a song in her heart. She had done a good deed. The elderly lady was happy, and so too was the little girl. She now understood what her father meant when he said, "It is more blessed to give than to receive."

The little girl in this story has grown to adulthood and has attempted to build her personal and professional life on the values of compassion, empathy, sharing, giving, and focusing on the needs of others as modeled and taught by her mother and father. Vocationally, she has become a psychologist, in fact, the psychologist who writes this book. Thank you, Mom and Dad.

Permit me to share one other personal story to illustrate how values are taught and modeled. My family lived in a small mid-western town, where life was simple and people were trustworthy. Consistently, my parents left the back door of our two-story bungalow unlocked.

One Monday after Mom had washed and folded the laundry, we as a family went out for the afternoon. When we returned, each pair of Dad's clean socks had been taken from the laundry room, unfolded, and draped one after another up the steps going to the second story. Obviously, Dad's fun-loving brother Joe had been over. This was his calling card.

Decades have passed and we still smile to think of him. Over and over again, he modeled the values of humor, love, and strong family relationships. He consistently brought joy and happiness to those around him. His children and grandchildren demonstrate these same values in their lives and relationships today.

As you complete the first column of the Value Clarification Chart on page 24, think of your parents and others who have taught you various values. Record these values.

Then move to the second column and indicate the principles taught by your school and church. Think of your favorite and least favorite school and church school teachers. Why were they liked or disliked? What did they model or teach? Who is the minister, priest, or rabbi you most remember? Why? What was taught and modeled? What was the sermon or church service you most remember? Why? To help you complete this column, remember experiences, mottoes, rules, and behaviors that were rewarded.

Then move to the last and most important column, labeled *Self.* This section is for your own personal values. Take from the first and second columns the ones you have kept. If you have changed any of them, write them as they have been modified. Then, if some of the values discussed in this chapter fit for you, write them down in your column as well.

In order to help you clarify your values even further, think about the following categories and questions.

- Friends you have selected: What characteristics drew you to them? Their sense of humor? Their willingness to listen? Their sound advice? Each of these characteristics can be a value.

- Sports you enjoy: What is it that appeals to you? If you enjoy team sports, do you like teamwork? Cooperation? If you like individual sports, do you appreciate self-reliance? Time to be alone? Do you enjoy competition, or do you prefer activities that can be done together but without competition? Again, values underlie each of these.

- Hobbies you enjoy: What is it that appeals to you? If you appreciate reading, do you like learning? Relaxation? If you enjoy a stamp collection or baseball cards, do you like to trade, buy, and sell? Do you enjoy the solitary time spent on these collections, the business aspect, or both?

- Heroes and heroines you have selected: What about them do you most admire? If you appreciate Helen Keller, do you admire her determination to overcome seemingly insurmountable odds? If you esteem General Douglas MacArthur, do you value his patriotism, dedication, loyalty to his country, or his ability to plan strategically?

- Major decisions you have made in your life: On what grounds have you made them? If you volunteered your time at the hospital for the sake of medical exposure and experience, do you appreciate well-informed career decisions? If you worked to put yourself through school even though your parents were able to provide the money, do you value financial self-sufficiency and self-reliance?

- Major conflicts you have had in your life: Did you resign your position because your boss was critical and disrespectful? Was the pay among workers unequal even though the jobs were the same? Did you discontinue a long-standing friendship because your friend became a social climber, opinionated, or self-impressed?

Behind each of these questions lies a value. Review and consider your life, and clarify the underlying values. Look at your parents, other significant people in your life, school, church, friends, sports, hobbies, heroes and heroines, major decisions, and conflicts. Each of these can provide you with information about the values you have adopted. Some of these may be stronger than others. Some are non-negotiable, and some are negotiable. In order to distinguish between the two, put an asterisk (*) next to the ones that for you are non-negotiable.

As you read the remaining chapters, you may recognize other values and wish to add them to your column. Long after you have completed this book, you may become aware of other specific values and add them to your chart. This assignment takes time and deliberation.

Expend the effort necessary to clarify your list of values. It will pay off in terms of understanding yourself and your decision-making. With your non-negotiable values clearly in mind, you can select a partner whose values match. A careful choice can yield baseline compatibility and greatly reduce conflict.

The theory that opposites attract definitely does not apply in the area of values. In fact, the reverse is true. When the non-negotiable values mesh, compatibility is increased and conflict is decreased.

If you are already in a relationship and experience repeated conflict, it would be helpful to know both your own and your partner's non-negotiable values. Hence, it would be beneficial if your spouse would read this chapter and also do the value clarification assignment. For that purpose, an extra Value Clarification Chart is included. Then the two of you can compare your respective lists and identify specific differences.

One of the significant things about the concept of values is that the focus is on the principle or belief, not the person. Rather than downgrade your partner and conclude that your mate is inadequate, you can identify the differences in your non-negotiable values. There is not necessarily anything wrong with either of you as persons; you simply have one or more divergent non-negotiable values. When you realize this, you can constructively work with these value differences rather than point the finger of blame.

Value Clarification Chart

PARENTS	CHURCH/SCHOOL	SELF
1)	1)	1)
2)	2)	2)
3)	3)	3)
4)	4)	4)
5)	5)	5)
6)	6)	6)
7)	7)	7)
8)	8)	8)
9)	9)	9)
		10)
		11)
		12)
		13)
		14)
		15)
		16)
		17)
		18)

*Put an asterisk next to the values that for you are non-negotiable.

Value Clarification Chart

PARENTS	CHURCH/SCHOOL	SELF
1)	1)	1)
2)	2)	2)
3)	3)	3)
4)	4)	4)
5)	5)	5)
6)	6)	6)
7)	7)	7)
8)	8)	8)
9)	9)	9)
		10)
		11)
		12)
		13)
		14)
		15)
		16)
		17)
		18)

*Put an asterisk next to the values that for you are non-negotiable.

VALUES: BRIDGING AND MODIFYING

If, as you and your partner complete your respective Value Clarification Charts, you find that your difference is between two non-negotiable values, you can bridge that difference with understanding. Because your values are non-negotiable, in all likelihood neither of you is going to change. You will simply need to accept this variance. If you argue, nag, and try to convince your spouse to change, the conflict and emotional distance will increase, while the non-negotiable value itself will not change. Generally, the only workable alternative with two divergent non-negotiable values is to bridge the difference with understanding. Kelly and Kevin's situation will serve to illustrate.

While Kelly has a non-negotiable value about straight-forwardness, Kevin has a non-negotiable value about tact. Since both are non-negotiable, Kelly and Kevin need to bridge this difference with understanding. They need to agree to disagree. Kelly must come to accept that whether she and Kevin are alone or with others, he will work diligently to be tactful and kind. Although Kelly may sometimes think the meaning is lost because of the carefulness with which the message is delivered, she must appreciate this style as non-negotiable for Kevin.

On the other hand, whether Kelly and Kevin are together or with others, Kelly calls it the way she sees it. Kevin may think she borders on being insensitive, but a similar bridge of understanding is necessary on his part. Since they love each other, treasure the relationship, and want to reduce the conflict, they agree that both of them are free to express themselves as they see fit. Each tries to accept and adjust to the other's style. They work to bridge with understanding the difference in their non-negotiable values related to straightforwardness versus tact.

To illustrate, let's imagine that Kelly and Kevin attend a party. Their friends Tracy and Terry share with them that they have marital problems.

Terry: "We have talked about separation but are reluctant because of the children."

Kevin: "It sounds like you are really struggling. Have you considered professional counseling?"

Terry: "We have talked about it."

Kelly: "Talked about it! You need to get a move on it. Problems like yours do not solve themselves."

Both Kelly and Kevin are concerned about Tracy and Terry's marriage, but they address the concern quite differently. Kevin is gentle and tactful. Kelly is bold and straightforward. If their styles are non-negotiable for both, they need to accept each other's method of communication and bridge this difference with understanding.

For most differences in non-negotiable values, bridging can be done. However, there are some exceptions. For example, if you support monogamy and sexual fidelity and your partner believes in open marriage and sexual freedom, these differences are difficult if not impossible to bridge. Over time, these opposite non-negotiable values destroy the relationship. However, with concerted effort, the majority of differences can be bridged with understanding.

A difference in values becomes considerably easier if it is between a principle which is non-negotiable for one of you and negotiable for the other. With the example about tact versus boldness, if Kevin's value is non-negotiable and Kelly's is negotiable, Kelly can modify her straight-forwardness from time to time for Kevin's sake. If there are certain circumstances where this is particularly important to him, on those occasions she can choose her words more carefully and thoughtfully.

In order for this adjustment to be possible, both Kelly and Kevin need to have a common understanding of negotiable and non-negotiable values and have a shared awareness that this is a negotiable value for Kelly. Then, either before or at the party, Kevin can ask Kelly to be more thoughtful and less direct.

Here is a scenario which could occur on the way to the party.

Kevin:	"I hear by the grapevine that Terry and Tracy have marital problems. If they share this sensitive information with us tonight, how should we handle it?"
Kelly:	"You know me. I'll call it the way I see it. Do you have any problem with that?"
Kevin:	"I appreciate your willingness to discuss this before we see them, because this is one of those times when I would really like both of us to be gentle and understanding."
Kelly:	"You mean you want me to soft-sell my reaction?"
	Kevin and Kelly laugh together.
Kevin:	"That's it. Soft-sell. Thanks, honey. This means a great deal to me."
Kelly:	(With a smile.) "Only for you, my dear."

A second scenario could happen at the party and in the midst of the conversation with Tracy and Terry.

Terry:	"We have talked about separation but are reluctant because of the children."
Kevin:	"It sounds like you are really struggling. Have you considered professional counseling?"

Terry:	"We have talked about it."

Kelly:	"Talked about it! You need to get a move on it. Problems like yours do not solve themselves."

Kevin gives Kelly's hand a loving squeeze.

Kevin:	"Honey, let's be as gentle, supportive, and understanding as possible. These are difficult issues and decisions."

Kelly:	"I hear you. I sometimes come on strong, but it's because I care. We really love you two and want your marriage to succeed."

This type of modification for specific circumstances can greatly reduce conflict. Kelly can alter her behavior from time to time. Although her basic value about straightforwardness probably will not change, it is negotiable. Accordingly, Kevin and Kelly have two options: to bridge with understanding or modify in specific situations.

VALUE DIFFERENCES: IMPACT ON A RELATIONSHIP

With all of these concepts in mind, let's return to our two couples, Tricia and Tom, and Betsy and Ben. As you may recall, their respective reunions were scheduled for the summer. As the last few weeks of the second semester passed, each couple set specific dates and made the related plans.

Although Tom wished to drive to Washington, D.C., Tricia dissuaded him. It was a disadvantage to have a vehicle in the city because there was limited space to park. Although Tom thoroughly enjoyed driving and had wanted to see the countryside between Wisconsin and Washington, D.C., Tricia was very clear about the no-vehicle policy.

Therefore, on the appointed day, Tom flew into Reagan Washington National Airport. Tricia met him and assisted him as he got his luggage. She looked beautiful, although her Florida tan had long since disappeared. Off to the subway they went. Fortunately, it was Saturday, but even so there was a significant press of people and no one was particularly polite.

"Mom and Dad are eager to meet you," Tricia began as they settled into the subway seats. "They are glad you are staying with us. They both are home this weekend, but Mom is involved with a major case. She'll take the train to New York early Monday morning and will be gone all week. Dad has a late dinner meeting on Wednesday evening. So let's make the most of this weekend with them." Tom listened and silently considered this lifestyle so different from his parents'.

When they arrived at the Georgetown townhouse, Tom was impressed with how close and compact the homes seemed to be. How different from the open, spacious countryside on which his parental home was situated. Tricia unlocked and opened the front door.

As they walked into the living room, Tom noticed the two tall windows that looked out onto the tiny but perfect backyard. The room itself was decorated with French Provincial furniture. Each piece was color-coordinated and elegant. Classical music played in the background. Tom felt as if he had entered one of those pictures in the *House Beautiful* or *Better Homes and Gardens* magazines.

As he walked closer to the windows, he could see the red brick patio surrounded by blooming, colorful flowers. "Beautiful," was all he said–very quiet for Tom. As he turned, he noticed there were fresh flowers in a cut crystal vase on the dining room table. He felt as if he were in another world filled with class and culture.

Tricia guided him upstairs to the guest room. "Get settled and then let's plan our week. I'll meet you back in the living room."

Tom was contemplative as he unpacked. Was this the fun-loving, carefree woman he had met in Ft. Lauderdale? The one in the pictures from the photo booth? This place was beautiful. Everything was perfect–perfectly manicured backyard, perfectly decorated and coordinated interior, perfect and elegant in every way. What was he, a Wisconsin farm boy, doing here? He paused and sat down on the edge of the bed.

"Hmm," he thought. "I had better make the best of this, redefine it as an adventure, face it with my usual spunk and enthusiasm. There has never been a situation I could not handle, and this will not be the first."

He stood up and brushed out the wrinkles in the bedspread. People in this class probably did not sit on their beds and wrinkle the bedspreads. Sure enough, there was a satin-covered lounge chair as well as a petite period desk and chair in the corner. He made a mental note not to sit on the bed again.

He collected himself and resumed his buoyant air. He found Tricia in the living room. "Okay, madam, lead on. I'm ready to conquer this town, as well as the hearts of your parents."

And so the week began. The four of them went to a Greek restaurant on Saturday evening and then to a play at the Kennedy Center. On Sunday, they attended the late morning service at the National Cathedral and then went to the country club for brunch. Tricia's parents introduced Tom to their friends. Some of the names and faces Tom recognized as people he had read about in the newspaper. Impressive, to say the least. Tom was charming. Tricia, as well as her mother and father, was impressed with his charisma.

When the weekend with her parents was over, Tricia and Tom relaxed in T-shirts and blue jeans. The agenda for the week was to sight-see every waking moment. They covered Washington, D.C., tourist style: the Lincoln, Washington, and Jefferson memorials; the Capitol Building, Supreme Court, Library of Congress, National Gallery of Art, and Museum of Natural History; and a tour of the White House.

They got up early and went to bed late. Each morning they began by drinking strong, steaming coffee. Each evening ended in the living room with soft music and intimate conversation. The romance blossomed.

At the end of the week, Tom flew back to Wisconsin. His thoughts ran crisscross in rather disjointed fashion. Tricia was wonderful: attractive, well-educated, career-oriented, and humorous. She was everything a man could want. She probably would join one of the most prestigious public accounting firms and eventually make a large income, travel extensively, and expect the type of lifestyle she had always known. Her family was wealthy and cosmopolitan.

Although he had thoroughly enjoyed his week of living in luxury, he was a farm boy headed for a career in veterinary medicine. He would work with farmers, field hands, and large animals. How could this combination ever work? Their personalities meshed, but what about their priorities, lifestyles, and values?

A few weeks later, Betsy and Ben were reunited as well. From National Airport, they took the subway to Landover, Maryland. Upon their arrival at the house, Mitch, the family schnauzer, eagerly met them at the door. He barked enthusiastically. Mitch, like Betsy's parents, loved visitors. Betsy laughed about how Mitch had taken on the personality and characteristics of his owners.

Betsy's mother greeted Ben warmly. After a brief conversation, she returned to the meal preparation while Betsy showed Ben upstairs to his room. In this rather spacious colonial home, there was always room for one more. It was Friday, and Betsy's father would be home shortly to do the chicken kabobs on the grill and to plan the weekend.

Ben unpacked, came downstairs, and offered to set the picnic table on the deck. Just then, her father arrived. Since he taught the summer session, he came in with briefcase in hand. Introductions were made, and Betsy's dad set Ben to work grilling the kabobs while he changed into more casual clothes.

When he returned to check on Ben's progress, he asked, "What is the plan? Do you want to sail or sight-see this weekend?"

Betsy looked at Ben. "Let's sail this weekend and sight-see next week. That way the four of us can be together for a few days. Ben and I will see the city next week."

"Great," Betsy's dad said with a broad smile of approval. He loved sailing, and a crew of four was perfect. "After dinner, let's pack the car and go down tonight. All you need is a bathing suit, bermudas, and a sweatshirt, Ben. We have everything else on board."

"Sounds good to me. I'm not a seasoned sailor, but I'm eager to learn," Ben responded.

The weekend was warm and sunny, with perfect wind conditions. The four of them sailed all day Saturday. In the evening, they bought fresh fish at the market near the dock and had seafood and fresh vegetables for dinner as they watched the sun set. They topped off the evening with a walk to town and a frozen yogurt.

On Sunday morning, they decided to attend the worship service at the United States Naval Academy. Since Ben did not have long pants, he wore trousers belonging to Betsy's father. Fortunately, her dad had a pair with an elastic waistband because Ben was a size or two smaller. The pants were a little short, but Ben just laughed good-naturedly about it. The shirt he borrowed fit no better. However, the brightly colored tie was perfect. After the service, they had a quick lunch and headed back out to sea. It was nearly midnight by the time they got back to Landover. Everyone was sunburned, exhausted, and happy.

On Monday morning, Betsy and Ben scrambled eggs, brewed coffee, reminisced about the weekend, and planned the week: a tour of the White House, the Capitol Building, and the Kennedy Center; a visit to the monuments and the Smithsonian; and a drive to Old Town in Alexandria. The week was filled to the brim. When it ended, both Betsy and Ben were exhausted but pleased with themselves. They had seen it all.

As Ben flew back to Wisconsin, he had warm memories and sincere appreciation for Betsy and her parents. Her family, like his, enjoyed being together and had many shared interests. And Mitch really was a good ambassador. He and his owners loved people and were very inclusive. Ben had felt thoroughly at home.

Imagine that Betsy and Ben complete their respective Value Clarification Charts and Tricia and Tom do likewise. Let's see how closely each couple's values mesh.

Betsy's Value Clarification Chart

PARENTS	CHURCH/SCHOOL	BETSY'S VALUES

1) Education
2) Service to others
3) A comfortable home
4) Family time and shared
     activities
	1) Involvement in the
	     Catholic Church
	2) Compassion for others
		*1) Education
		*2) Service to others
		*3) Adequate funds for a
		     comfortable home and
		     lifestyle
		*4) Quality family time
		*5) Continued involvement
		     in the Catholic Church
		*6) Compassion for others
		
		*Non-negotiable value

Ben's Value Clarification Chart

PARENTS	CHURCH/SCHOOL	BEN'S VALUES

1) Education
2) Service to others
3) A comfortable home
4) Home and family time
	1) Involvement in the
	     Baptist Church
	2) Love of God and others
		*1) Education
		*2) Service to others
		*3) Adequate funds for a
		     comfortable home and
		     lifestyle
		*4) Quality family time
		  5) Continued involvement
		     in the Baptist Church
		*6) Love of God and others
		
		*Non-negotiable value

As is apparent, Betsy and Ben have similar values. No wonder Ben felt so comfortable with Betsy and her family.

Betsy and Ben's values mesh well. They both are focused on service professions, and both are committed to helpfulness and compassion. They seek religious as well as professional expression of their values. Church involvement is important. Each comes from a close-knit family and wishes to continue this pattern. Their negotiable and non-negotiable values are congruent. There is little if any need to bridge or modify.

With Tricia and Tom the situation is quite different, as the following charts reveal.

Tricia's Value Clarification Chart

PARENTS	CHURCH/SCHOOL	TRICIA'S VALUES
1) Education and professional success	1) Episcopalian tradition	*1) Educational and professional success
2) Money and material possessions		*2) Money and material possessions
3) Prestige		*3) Prestige
4) High-profile personal and professional connections		*4) High-profile personal and professional connections
5) Cultured lifestyle		*5) Cultured lifestyle
		*6) Residence in a major city on the East Coast
		7) Episcopalian tradition

*Non-negotiable value

Tom's Value Clarification Chart

PARENTS	CHURCH/SCHOOL	TOM'S VALUES
1) Agrarian lifestyle	1) Involvement in the Assemblies of God Church	*1) The necessary education to reach vocational goals
2) Success as measured by cooperative and helpful human relationships	2) Dependence on God	*2) Agrarian lifestyle
3) Enough money to live comfortably		*3) Service to others
		*4) Compassionate and helpful to animals
		5) Enough money to live comfortably
		6) Continued involvement in the Assemblies of God Church
		*7) Dependence on God

*Non-negotiable value

If Tricia and Tom pursue the relationship, they face many challenges. Tricia has several non-negotiable values that Tom does not share, and vice versa. Tricia not only comes from a wealthy family but also eventually will command a high salary herself.

Tricia's values about money, material possessions, and a cultured lifestyle are non-negotiable. Fortunately, Tom's value regarding wealth is negotiable. Although Tom can make a very good living, his primary commitment is to farmers, animals, and the agrarian lifestyle. However, if he marries Tricia, he will need to bridge with understanding this value difference. He'll need to increase the worth he places on money. With the lifestyle Tricia desires, Tom will need to earn a high income and live upscale. He must negotiate his financial and lifestyle values.

In Tom's agrarian background, he and his fellow farmers have experienced a high degree of dependence on each other and the Lord. Therefore, his personal relationship with God is very deeply ingrained. However, his particular denominational affiliation is negotiable. The same is true for Tricia. Therefore, religious affiliation may be resolvable, although it will be a challenge due to the difference in style of worship. Their experiences have been quite different.

The greatest challenge will be the issue of geographic location, with its implications for their respective careers. According to their value charts, both are rather inflexible about the section of the country in which they wish to live. Their location will influence their practices and respective clientele. On this issue, each has a non-negotiable value. By definition, non-negotiable values cannot be negotiated.

Being a successful CPA in a high-profile public accounting firm on the East Coast is non-negotiable for Tricia. Having a large-animal practice which is associated with farm country and the agrarian lifestyle is non-negotiable for Tom. Will Tricia practice in either a branch office of a major firm or a smaller, less prestigious firm so that Tom can have a large-animal practice? Will Tom do a small-animal practice so Tricia can affiliate with a big-name firm in a large metropolitan area? Could Tom and Tricia live near enough to a major city for Tricia to practice with a prestigious firm and far enough into the country for Tom to have a large-animal practice? In all likelihood, there will be considerable stress around the issue of geographic location and the subsequent nature of their respective practices.

Geographic location with the corresponding implications for their individual careers is a thorny issue. The skill of compromise, which will be reviewed in Chapter 3, is especially relevant to this situation. We will discuss Tricia and Tom's value conflicts in greater detail in that chapter.

For Tricia and Tom, conflict is inherent from the beginning. They will need to bridge and modify their differences fairly early in the relationship. In contrast, Betsy and Ben begin with a compatible and conflict-free foundation. Since their values mesh, they can move on to other aspects of their relationship.

In summary, then, in order to design a successful marriage, it is important to select a spouse who shares your non-negotiable values. When the match is close, compatibility increases and conflict decreases. If your choice has already been made, identify any non-negotiable value that does not mesh, and work to bridge or to modify.

CHAPTER 2

EMPATHY

After their respective visits, both couples corresponded. Each had one more reunion. Tricia flew to Wisconsin to be with Tom in early August, and Betsy came out later in the month.

Tom had mixed feelings as he drove to the airport. He was eager to see Tricia, but nervous about how she'd like the Midwest and the agrarian lifestyle. He had just washed and vacuumed his old pickup truck. He didn't want it to look like the dirty farm vehicle it had been a few days earlier. He parked and went inside to await her arrival.

When she walked into the terminal, she looked stunning. Her smile was radiant as she embraced and kissed Tom. Any misgivings melted.

Tom had coached his parents about their appropriate behavior and appearance while Tricia visited. They agreed to meet his standards, but with the clear understanding that to run a dairy farm was very time-intensive and not always neat and tidy. They also pointed out that she had a responsibility to blend in and adjust. His parents tried to balance consideration with reality. They were firm and forthright. Tom, like everyone else in their world, always knew where he stood.

When Tom and Tricia drove up the long driveway to the house, the farm looked like a picture postcard: white two-story home, large red barn, and black and white Holsteins in the pasture. The foliage was lush and green; the white fence looked precise. Sadie, the family collie, lay quietly on the front porch and raised her head as they approached. She was old now and no longer rose to greet visitors.

Tom saw all of this with new eyes as Tricia sat next to him. This farm was God's grandeur. He loved it regardless of how Tricia reacted.

"It's beautiful," she said with awe in her voice. "Absolutely beautiful. No wonder you love it here."

Tom and Tricia parked near the house and entered through the side door into the kitchen. Sadie came in with them and nuzzled Tricia's hand. It was lunch time, and Tom's mother was in the kitchen. She wore her light blue cobbler's apron over her blue jeans and red plaid shirt.

She broke into a broad grin and clasped Tricia's hand between both of hers. "Welcome to Homestead Acres. We are very pleased you could come. We love this farm and hope you will too. Tom has given us glowing reports about you." She turned toward Tom and said, "Please, show Tricia upstairs to her room."

Tom obliged. As they walked through the house, Tricia was struck by the high ceilings and the lacquered floors covered by large, colorful area rugs. As they walked upstairs, she noticed the carpeting–a tight-woven muted stripe laid like a runner up the center of the stairs, with wood exposed on either side. The guest room was small and tucked in between the other bedrooms. This house felt like a place out of *Huckleberry Finn*.

Tom broke into her thoughts: "Feel free to get settled. Then come down for lunch. Everyone will join us—Dad and the other farmhands."

"Will Ben be here?" asked Tricia.

"Not this week. He's looking for an apartment in Madison for the fall semester, but he sends his warm regards. He says you'll be a farmerette by the end of the week." They both laughed and embraced.

Tom left and she unpacked. As she hung her clothes in the small closet, she noticed the narrow closet door and the door knob which seemed like an antique, bigger and more ornate than current hardware. This farm house must have been in the family for generations, she thought. It is old and well worn.

Briefly, she stood before the window which looked over the fields. She could see the black and white cows as they grazed. She was struck by the difference between the precision of the small backyard in Georgetown and the patchwork quilt of the seemingly endless countryside in which the herd slowly moved.

"Amazing," she said softly to herself as she slid her empty suitcase under the bed. She guessed that is where it belonged since the closet was too small and there was no other place to put it. Every nook and cranny was filled. There was a wooden rocker in the corner, and a nightstand with drawers on each side of the bed.

As she came down the stairs, she heard the others enter the kitchen. After introductions, they sat down like a large family at the huge round oak table in the center of the kitchen. In addition to Tom, his parents, and herself, there were four rather sweaty field hands.

The menu was very Midwestern: sweet corn, cole slaw, barbecues, and fresh blueberry pie a la mode. No concern for fat grams, Tricia smiled to herself. This was so different from Washington, D.C., where it seemed that almost everyone was weight and health conscious, ate alfalfa sprouts, and went to a fitness club to exercise.

The conversation was lively–about Tricia, her family, the trip, the morning milking, farm prices, and local farmers. It was easy and free-flowing. She felt included. Sadie lay contentedly nearby, waiting for a scrap under the table. Tom obliged, as Tricia knew he would. She smiled at him.

When lunch was over, the men got up and filed out the back door. They put their soiled caps back on as they left. She hadn't noticed, but each man had a baseball cap tucked into the back pocket of his overalls. Now she understood why Tom and Ben had often worn baseball caps in Florida.

As everyone resumed activity, Tom's mother started to clear the table and Tom began to assist. She took her cue from him and concluded she was more family than guest. She picked up several plates.

"Let us finish, Mom. Feel free to go back to your chores," Tom said. As Tricia discovered, Tom's mother balanced the books, bought and sold the animals, and kept track of the bloodlines of the stock. Those responsibilities, along with cooking, were more than a full-time job.

Tom's dad shopped for groceries when he was in town for supplies. He coordinated all of the men, fed the animals, milked, repaired the farm equipment, and worked alongside of the vet with animal health problems and deliveries. With such a large herd, they both kept very busy.

Tom's mother quickly accepted Tom's offer and disappeared into her office adjacent to the kitchen. This location was ideal. Her major responsibilities, food preparation and recordkeeping, could be coordinated. It was apparent to Tricia that this was a smooth, well-run operation. Tom's parents handled it comfortably. She thought to herself, this is the heartland of America. This is what the Midwest is all about.

Tom interrupted her thoughts. "It's hot. Let's take out the ski boat this afternoon. Do you water ski?" Tom asked.

"No. I only downhill ski," responded Tricia.

"Do you want to learn?" queried Tom.

"Sure. I'm game. There's a good reason Betsy and I are called the undaunted duo," she laughed cheerfully.

They finished the dishes, changed their clothes, attached the boat and trailer to the back of the pickup truck, and headed to Lake Winnebago. Upon arrival, they launched the boat and were off. They laughed as the wind began to snarl Tricia's hair. They raced around the lake at full throttle. Eventually, they dropped anchor in Tom's favorite bayou and went swimming. While they dried off in the boat, they munched potato chips, drank pop, and talked. They didn't need to plan as they had when they were in Washington, D.C. They could simply do whatever they wished.

"Are you ready to water ski?" Tom asked.

"Yes. Let's do it," responded Tricia eagerly.

Tom pulled up the anchor, started the engine, and drove toward a protected, shallow location near shore. As they traveled, Tom explained the principles of water skiing. Tricia listened and repeated his directions to double-check that she fully understood.

Upon arrival at the desired spot, Tom put the boat into neutral. He attached the tow rope to the stern, dropped the skis into the water, and gave Tricia a life jacket. She slipped overboard. She put on the skis and got into position with the line between them. When she was ready, Tom accelerated. Tricia fell. Around he went so she could reclaim the line and replace the skis. The process was repeated. Again she tried and fell. After several attempts, she became frustrated. With intense disgust, she quit. As she got into the boat, she was furious.

"What a ridiculous sport. Who would want to do this anyway? Bimbos, I guess. Forget it. Is this your idea of a joke?" Tricia asked.

"Sometimes it can take a little time to learn. You looked particularly good on the second and third tries. I know you feel discouraged. I did too when I learned. You certainly gave it your best shot," Tom said empathetically.

"This is a ridiculous sport. I won't try it again. I hope your other ideas aren't as bad as this one," Tricia said with blame and sarcasm in her voice.

Her comments stung, but Tom tried to shrug them off. After all, it had been a long trip and she was probably tired. Besides, people probably didn't water ski in Washington, D.C. Perhaps it was a bad idea.

Although Tom enjoyed the sport himself, he didn't ask Tricia to drive the boat so he could ski. He didn't want to flaunt his expertise. Instead, they did a little more sightseeing on the lake and then put the boat back on the trailer and returned home.

Although Tricia's visit was only four days, Thursday through Sunday, Tom wanted her to experience his lifestyle. Thursday and skiing had gone poorly, but he had great hopes for the remaining three days.

On Friday, they rode horses. Tricia indicated that she preferred English to Western saddle. Friday night, they danced at the Homespun Disco, which featured country and western music. She made the point that homespun certainly captured the flavor and quality of the music. On Saturday, they went to a cattle auction. She stomped her feet several times to get the dirt off her shoes.

On Sunday, they attended a worship service at his church. The congregation clapped, sang, shared, prayed, and listened to the sermon. The service went on for nearly two hours. Afterwards almost everyone stayed for coffee, punch, and cookies. The children played while the adults discussed the local news.

As they drove back to the farm, Tom indicated that he thought the service was particularly inspirational. Tricia was silent. She thought it resembled a revival or tent meeting, something she had read about but had had no desire to experience. She found it very unstructured and freewheeling, very different from the liturgical style of the Episcopalian tradition. She felt out of place and miserable but said nothing. She had a migraine headache by the time they got home. She went to bed for the remainder of the day.

On Monday morning, Tom took her to the airport. He felt disappointed and inadequate. She appeared eager to return to a more familiar lifestyle. Oshkosh, Wisconsin, and Washington, D.C., were lifestyles apart.

Meanwhile, during these same few days, Ben was in Madison looking for an apartment near the various hospitals and clinics at which he would do his clinical training. He found a furnished studio. It was small but adequate.

When he called Betsy and told her about it, she volunteered to come to Wisconsin earlier than planned in order to help him move. She said she could make the place cozy. He enthusiastically agreed. They decided to spend some time with his family and then drive to Madison and organize the apartment.

When the day arrived, Ben sat nervously in the airport. Would their time together go well? He had the same goal as Tom had had, to have Betsy experience life in the Midwest.

Her plane landed. As the passengers entered the terminal, she walked toward Ben. Rather than embracing him, she handed him a book and smiled mischievously.

He looked down and realized it was a manual on the principles of sailing, published by the United States Coast Guard. "It's from Dad. He said you should read it before the next visit so you can be the captain on our next family voyage. I think he is eager for the son he never had." Ben chuckled with obvious pleasure as he caught her up in his arms.

Immediately, they were into lively conversation about Betsy's trip, their respective summers, the apartment, and the plans for their time together. They talked uninterruptedly while they claimed Betsy's luggage and traveled to Ben's home.

Upon arrival, she saw his father mowing the lawn and his mother weeding the garden. "It's Dad's day off. Mom arranges to have the same day free so they can do yard work together. It's one of their hobbies. They thoroughly enjoy doing it." The pride in Ben's voice was apparent. He honked the horn as they drove into the driveway of the walkout ranch home.

His dad stopped the mower, and his mother removed her gardening gloves and the large straw hat which she wore as a shade from the sun. "Hello." "Welcome." Ben's parents spoke simultaneously, jumbling both greetings together. Everyone laughed at the coincidence. Ben made the introductions and then guided Betsy to her room while his parents finished the yard work.

All the bedrooms except the master suite were on the lower level. In the far corner was her room. There was a sliding door out to the wooded backyard. Although this home was in the city, it felt peaceful and private. As she settled in, she sat down in one of the two white deck chairs and gazed out. A small hummingbird fluttered in the nearby flower garden. "How beautiful," she thought as she got up and finished unpacking.

As she came upstairs, she could hear Ben and his parents as they talked. "We'd love to take the two of you to the Homespun Disco for dinner. We'll bow out before the dancing begins."

As Betsy entered the kitchen, Ben turned to her. Before he spoke, Betsy said, "Whatever you plan will be fine with me." That decided it.

After a quick shower and change of clothes, the four of them were off. The waitress obviously knew Ben and his parents. The banter was easy and lighthearted. As the evening wore on, the music started. The first song called for line dancing.

"Let's all four do it," said Betsy. Before Ben's dad could decline, Betsy grabbed him by the arm and headed for the dance floor. Ben and his mother enthusiastically followed. One dance led to another, and before they knew it the last number of the evening was played.

"What fun. Can't believe two old duffers like us can still dance until the wee hours of the morning," Ben's dad said as he winked at his wife. As they left and drove home, they chatted and laughed.

The next day was beautiful, warm and sunny, perfect for boating. Tom's pickup, with the boat and trailer attached, was parked next to the garage. Ben had made the necessary arrangements prior to Betsy's arrival.

After breakfast, Ben and Betsy headed for the lake and launched the boat. They toured, swam, and munched on snacks. Betsy did not know any more about skiing than Ben knew about sailing, but she came with an equally open attitude. However, she, like Tricia, had difficulty learning. After several attempts, she shouted to Ben, "OK. I surrender. I give up. White flag. Truce."

As she got into the boat, she feigned a faint. "I am done in, shot, kaput. If you are in search of a water-skiing companion, I am not it." She stopped, paused, and said seriously, "Are you disappointed? I really can't seem to get coordinated."

"No. I am not disappointed. It took me many tries over several weeks. Tom thought I was a hopeless case. To learn a new sport can be a real trial," he said empathetically.

She smiled, kissed him, and said, "Thanks. This is one of the reasons I love you. You are always so understanding."

He missed whatever followed the words "I love you." Had she said she loved him? She was already occupied with rewinding the tow rope, so he'd have to check this out later.

The next day they rode horses. She informed him that she was accustomed to an English rather than Western saddle, but she'd give it her best effort. They had fun.

On Sunday they attended church. Although the Protestant service was different from the Mass, Betsy thoroughly enjoyed the fact that they sang several of the same songs so many miles from her home church. Christianity felt so predictable, global, and secure. She was glad Ben and his family were active Christians like her family.

After brunch, Ben and Betsy packed the car and headed for Madison. They chatted and laughed. However, as they got closer to the city, Ben became very quiet. Betsy waited. She hoped he would share, but he didn't.

She gently started the conversation. "Tell me your thoughts. You seem very meditative."

"No big deal," he responded. She felt a little put off. She too got quiet–and angry. After a few minutes, she tried again.

"Ben, what is on your mind? I'd like to be supportive if you'd let me."

"I told you it's no big deal. Don't pry," Ben said sternly. He fell back into silence.

Several miles passed and Betsy fumed. Finally, she popped her top. "Look, Ben, I came out here to help you move. I have other things to do, but I want to be supportive of you. A transition as major as this has got to be difficult. Talk to me," she commanded.

"You're right," he said sharply. "It is difficult. What if I can't handle the practical part of this? What if I am really not cut out to be a physical therapist? What if this plan is a big mistake?" His voice trailed off. He looked overwhelmed and disconsolate.

"Sure, you have second thoughts. I wonder about teaching too sometimes. I guess if either of us makes a mistake, we'll try something else. Until we are proven to be wrong, however, let's assume we are on course." Betsy's voice softened as she went on.

"No matter what you decide to do vocationally, I'll still admire you and care deeply for you. Whether you become a physical therapist or something else, I am on your side." She squeezed his hand.

Ben was thrown off track again. She said "admire and care deeply." That could border on love. It was time to nail this down.

"Could we switch topics for a few minutes?" Ben asked. He didn't wait for her response. "Let's discuss our relationship." Suddenly Ben seemed re-energized. Betsy was taken aback.

They began a discussion which continued throughout the remainder of the drive and on into the time they organized Ben's apartment. They acknowledged that they were serious about each other and reached a clear understanding about the nature and direction of the relationship.

In contrast to Tricia and Tom, who concluded their time together with emotional distance and ambivalence, Betsy and Ben were unequivocally committed to each other. Not only did their non-negotiable values mesh, but they also had the ability to empathetically support each other and get over the rough spots. Empathy is the second component in the design for an enduring relationship.

DEFINITION

Empathy is the ability to listen to another with heartfelt understanding, to put aside your own feelings and connect with somebody else's. It requires you to get outside of yourself. There is an old saying: you can't know what someone else's life is like until you have walked a mile in the other's moccasins. Empathy is the ability to walk in someone else's moccasins. You intuit what the other person feels. You experience the other's joy, disappointment, or pain as if it were your own.

To understand empathy more fully, let's contrast it with sympathy. With sympathy, you intellectually understand the other's pain or problem and you feel sorry for or compassionate about that person's situation. You express in words and actions your consolation or support. Sympathy means you extend care and concern as you do with a handshake of sympathy at the funeral home. However, emotionally you are one step removed.

As noted above, with empathy you emotionally are in the other's shoes. You directly feel and experience the other's sadness, hurt, or loss. The pain is felt as if it were your own. Empathy is subjective and heartfelt.

An example will demonstrate the difference between the two. Imagine a tragedy in which your friends' child is killed in an automobile accident. With sympathy, you intellectually realize their loss. You go to the funeral home and give your condolences. You tell your friends that you feel sorry. However, you are one step removed from actually feeling their grief and pain. Sympathy is intellectual and objective.

In contrast, with empathy you emotionally feel their loss. When you walk into the funeral home, you are gripped with your friends' pain. You experience their grief as if it were your own. You are sad and overwhelmed with memories of this dear child. You realize how shattered and empty life has become. Their loss is sensed as if it were yours. You subjectively experience the emptiness and devastation. You walk in your friends' moccasins. Empathy is emotional and subjective.

With sympathy, you intellectually know that the child has died and you objectively give your regrets. With empathy, you not only know but also feel the grief. Your friends' loss is your loss. Your friends' pain is your pain. Subjectively, you are in the same emotional space.

HEAD AND HEART

In order to comprehend more fully how sympathy and empathy work, it is important to appreciate how we operate internally as individuals. It is essential to understand that each of us lives life on two primary levels, namely, the head and heart levels.

The head is the logical, intellectual, thoughtful part. It is where the shoulds and oughts, the rules and regulations about life are stored. For example, you intellectually know your friends' child died and realize you should go to the funeral home to extend your sympathy. That would be appropriate behavior.

The other is the heart level. Your heart is the center of your feelings, wants, and needs. You feel devastated when you learn that your friends' child died. You want to go to the funeral home and support them during this difficult time.

The diagram that follows illustrates the content of both levels.

Head and Heart

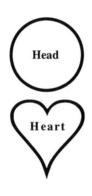

1. Logic, intellect, thoughts
2. Shoulds, oughts
3. Rules, regulations

1. Emotions
2. Feelings
3. Wants and needs

INTERNAL CONNECTEDNESS

Each part has a different perspective. The head holds the rules and regulations, shoulds and oughts for appropriate living. The heart feels the wants, needs, and emotions.

In order for a person to function fully, these two levels must be connected and be able to work together as a team. Your head and heart need to dialogue freely. The arrow in the diagram which follows illustrates the internal connectedness required between the two levels.

Internal Connectedness

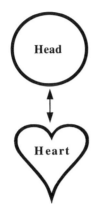

1. Logic, intellect, thoughts
2. Shoulds, oughts
3. Rules, regulations

1. Emotions
2. Feelings
3. Wants and needs

INTERNAL PROBLEM-SOLVING

It should be noted that, by their very nature, the head and heart have different perspectives. Therefore, when they are in conflict, they need to discuss and problem-solve together.

To illustrate, imagine that you are scheduled to co-chair a business meeting during the same time slot as your child's third-grade play. The head and heart have conflicting perspectives on this situation.

Your head states, "I should attend this business meeting because my partner and I worked out this presentation together." Your heart responds, "I want to attend my child's third-grade play. Such an event happens only once in a lifetime."

No matter which part begins the internal dialogue, each must have ample opportunity to state its perspective while the other listens. Once this has been done, they together move to the next step. They generate options and ultimately make and execute a decision.

With the example about the business meeting versus the third-grade play, after adequate dialogue between the head and heart, alternatives are developed. For example, I could ask my partner to do

the presentation while I attend the play. I could reschedule the
meeting. I could ask my spouse to videotape the play and then we
could view it as a family at a later time. After generating the options,
a choice can be made and action taken. This internal problem-
solving process can be diagrammed as follows.

Internal Problem-Solving

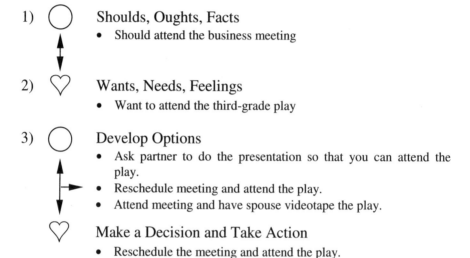

1) ◯   Shoulds, Oughts, Facts
          • Should attend the business meeting

2) ♡   Wants, Needs, Feelings
          • Want to attend the third-grade play

3) ◯   Develop Options
          • Ask partner to do the presentation so that you can attend the
            play.
          • Reschedule meeting and attend the play.
          • Attend meeting and have spouse videotape the play.

    ♡   Make a Decision and Take Action
          • Reschedule the meeting and attend the play.

This process of problem-solving or decision-making requires
internal connectedness wherein the head states the should and the
heart expresses the want. Then the two work together to develop
options and determine a suitable course of action. The eventual plan,
which in this example is to reschedule the meeting and attend the
play, needs to honor both the thoughts and the feelings.

EMPATHY BETWEEN PARTNERS

Now let's return to our discussion of empathy. As illustrated earlier
in this chapter, sympathy is primarily cognitive (Head): "I should go
to the funeral home and extend my condolences. It is the right thing

to do." Empathy is primarily emotional (Heart): "I feel their grief and devastation. I want to walk through this pain with them."

Empathy requires attachment to your heart. You must be in touch with your feelings. You need to be able to feel your own emotions before you can experience another's.

Likewise, in a marriage you need open and easy access to your own emotions before you can have the same type of access to your partner's. You need to feel and understand your own wants, needs, and feelings before you can experience your mate's. The same is true for your spouse. When internal connectedness is present within both partners, empathy between them can occur. The diagram that follows illustrates this principle.

Empathy Between Partners

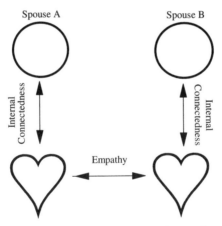

Empathy between spouses means your heart is connected to your partner's heart and vice versa. You and your mate interact at this level. Empathy is the second major component for an enduring marriage. When you and your spouse share empathy, your hearts are truly in sync. You are emotionally connected. Although each of you comprehends the facts, the feelings are the center of the communication. You emotionally walk in your mate's moccasins.

An example will serve to illustrate how empathy works in an intimate relationship. Mary's boss has given her a severe reprimand at work. She comes home and talks with her husband, George. She gives a brief overview of the events, but more important, she shares her feelings of embarrassment, hurt, and anger. George listens non-judgmentally and empathetically.

Mary:	"I feel awful. The boss told me my memo was difficult to read and understand. He said he would no longer attempt to decipher my penmanship. I told him that this note was simply an in-house memo for him, but it made no difference. He said I should either use the computer or dictate it so the secretary could type it. I felt embarrassed, angry, and hurt. I try so hard to be a responsible, conscientious employee."
George:	"I know you do. You really give your best effort to the company. I can appreciate how devastated you must have felt. "
Mary:	"I did. Fortunately, no one else was present, but even so, it's difficult to face tomorrow. Why try when all I do is get put down? What pain and disappointment."
George:	"It certainly is."
Mary:	"Oh well. I am home now so let's enjoy the evening. Things will look brighter in the morning. They always do. Thanks for listening."

Mary shares and George listens empathetically. He subjectively feels her pain. As George listens, her feelings of embarrassment, hurt, and anger decrease, and she begins to feel relief and deep appreciation that she has such a supportive, understanding, empathetic partner. She comes away feeling very loved.

With empathy, her spouse has enabled her to move from feeling angry and upset to feeling loved and supported. As George listens, subjectively feels her emotions, and says very little, he has facilitated not only the dissolution of her painful feelings but also an increase in the trust and intimacy that they share. Through his positive handling of her conflict at work, the two have grown closer. Empathy made the difference. Empathy turned Mary's emotional pain into increased intimacy between the two of them.

In this situation, George gave Mary empathy. At other times, she will give the same to him. Empathy between partners is one of the five components in the design for an enduring marriage.

CROSS-COMMUNICATION

In this example of George and Mary, there is virtually no head-to-head conversation. The entire dialogue is heart-to-heart. In a relationship, there is a time and a place for both head-to-head and heart-to-heart communication. The key factor is that a couple must be on the same level at the same time. Imagine what would have happened if George and Mary had mixed heart and head communication.

As Mary shared the feelings of her heart, George would have responded with the logic of his head. Instead of empathetically listening and feeling her pain, he would intellectually think about her difficult situation and try to fix it. He would generate ideas so that the conflict could be resolved. Cross-communication would result. Mary comes with her heart, and George responds with his head.

Empathy would stop instantly. For Mary, anger and resentment would occur. She would feel unheard, hurt, and discounted, as the following interaction illustrates.

Mary: "I feel awful. The boss told me my memo was difficult to read and understand. He said he would no longer attempt to decipher my penmanship. I told him that his note was simply an in-house memo for

him, but it made no difference. He said I should
either use the computer or dictate it so the secretary
could type it. I felt embarrassed, angry, and hurt. I
try so hard to be a responsible, conscientious
employee."

George: "He is right. Doing memos longhand is unwise. You
have several options. You could print rather than
write your memos, dictate them, or learn to use your
computer. I recommend that you do the latter. In
this day and age, it is wise to become computer
literate."

Imagine how Mary feels. She was already discouraged and
overwhelmed, and now George has added to it. She came to him
with her heart, and he responded with his head. She came to her
partner for empathy. She wanted heart-to-heart dialogue and instead
received head-level communication. As noted in the scenario where
empathy was given, when it was time to resolve the situation, she did
it herself. Mary needs her partner to give understanding, not
solutions.

She came to him for emotional support, and he gave her opinions
and recommendations. She feels unheard and unsupported and will
be reluctant to share something this painful in the future. For the
second time in one day, Mary feels incompetent. She leaves the
conversation deeply wounded.

In all likelihood, George feels the conversation was helpful. After
all, he gave Mary sound and appropriate advice. Who would argue
with the wisdom of becoming computer literate in this day and age?

This type of cross-communication is an all too common pattern in
marriage. In part, it relates to the societal focus on fixing. People,
whether professional, technical, or skilled labor, are paid large sums
of money to resolve issues and repair broken products. The better a
person solves problems, the higher the paycheck. When these fixers
get married, this strength is brought into the relationship. Whatever

the troublesome issue, it must be resolved. To simply listen seems inadequate. The fixer feels compelled to solve the problem, and therefore cross-communication results, and empathy is disallowed. Cross-communication can be diagrammed as follows:

Cross-Communication

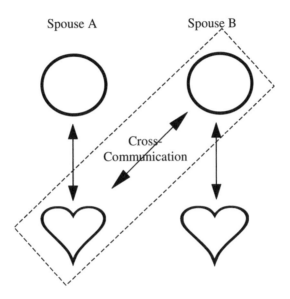

Spouse A   Spouse B

Cross-Communication

If head and heart communication are mixed, empathy is precluded. Resentment and hostility result. The spouse on the receiving end feels as if the pain and struggle are minimized and discounted. The focus is on the resolution of the issue rather than on the feelings related to the troublesome situation. As in the scenario with Mary and George, heart-to-heart communication is cut off, and hurt, anger, and resentment result.

As a rule of thumb, spouses want empathy, not advice, from their mates. They want a listening ear and an understanding heart. Whatever the troublesome issue, they will resolve it themselves. As demonstrated in the first scenario, Mary worked through the situation. She concluded that things would look brighter in the morning. Meanwhile, she left the discussion with a sense of closeness and appreciation for George and his support.

FEELING-WORD VOCABULARY

To avoid cross-communication, a partner must make certain to listen to the words used by the spouse. Words like *think, wonder,* and *opinion* are head words. Words like *anger, hurt,* and *fear* are heart words. Listen carefully to your spouse to discern if the conversation needs to be on the head or heart level.

In the first example, Mary used the words such as *embarrassment, angry, hurt, pain,* and *disappointment.* George listened and responded in kind. "I can appreciate how devastated you must have felt." George was very understanding and supportive. Both Mary and George stayed on the heart-to-heart level. Both used feeling words.

If you want empathy in your relationship, you need to know the language of feelings. In actuality, there is a feeling-word vocabulary, as the following list illustrates. Please add other words to the chart. The greater your vocabulary, the greater the probability you and your spouse will have the language and sensitivity to talk heart to heart and to exercise empathy.

Feeling-Word Vocabulary

Love	Enthusiasm
Anger	Hurt
Concern	Gratitude
Frustration	Disappointment
Joy	Sympathy
Fear	Disgust
Happiness	Warmth
Anxiety	Grief

Please add your own feeling words to this list.

To avoid cross-communication, you as partners must focus on being simultaneously on either the head or the heart level. Timing is critical. You must be on the same level at the same time for the same length of time.

If cross-communication is problematic in your relationship, be aware that this pattern can be changed. You will be able to modify it if you listen for heart versus head words. This is where the feeling-word vocabulary can be very helpful.

Another method to ensure effective heart-to-heart communication is to simply identify for your partner on which level you need to talk. For example, "George, I need to discuss my day at work on a heart-to-heart level." Remain on that level until one of you requests a change or shifts the vocabulary being used. If you use heart-type words or directly label the level on which you wish to talk, you will decrease cross-communication and increase empathy.

Now that we have discussed the importance of internal connectedness and empathy between partners, let's see what has been modeled for Betsy, Ben, Tricia, and Tom by their respective

parents. Betsy and Ben both come from homes where their parents
were in touch with their feelings and were able to share them with
their spouse.

Betsy's parents discussed their personal feelings related to their
profession, their relationship with each other, and life in general.
They often talked about the needs of the students in their respective
classrooms as well as concerns related to the families of these young
people. They shared, listened to each other, and gave mutual, non-
judgmental support. They felt comfortable with emotions.

Likewise with Ben's family. They were in touch with their own
and each other's feelings. They selected people-oriented occupations,
his mother as a practical nurse and his father as a salesperson, and
gave understanding to others as well.

Betsy and Ben had good role models for internal connectedness
and shared empathy. In fact, they both decided to build their
professional lives on compassion and service to others. Betsy chose
teaching, and Ben physical therapy.

When they went skiing together on Lake Winnebago, Betsy
clearly knew how she felt about her unsuccessful attempts, and Ben
was empathetic. The result was increased emotional intimacy
between them.

Betsy: She stopped, paused, and said seriously, "Are you
            disappointed? I really can't seem to get coordinated."

Ben: "No. I'm not disappointed. It took me many tries
            over several weeks. Tom thought I was a hopeless
            case. To learn a new sport can be a real trial," he said
            empathetically.

Betsy: She smiled, kissed him, and said, "Thanks. This is
            one of the reasons I love you. You are always so
            understanding." (p. 46)

Again, as the two of them traveled to Madison, internal connectedness, empathy, and increased emotional intimacy occurred, although initially the communication was rather angry and disjointed.

After brunch, Ben and Betsy packed the car and headed for Madison. They chatted and laughed. However, as they got closer to the city, Ben became very quiet. Betsy waited. She hoped he would share, but he didn't.

She gently started the conversation.

Betsy: "Tell me your thoughts. You seem very meditative."

Ben: "No big deal," he responded.

She felt a little put off. She too got quiet–and angry. After a few minutes she decided to try again.

Betsy: "Ben, what is on your mind? I'd like to be supportive if you'd let me."

Ben: "I told you it's no big deal. Don't pry," Ben said sternly. He fell back into silence.

Several miles passed and Betsy fumed. Finally, she popped her top.

Betsy: "Look Ben, I came out here to help you move. I have other things to do but I want to be supportive of you. A transition as major as this has got to be difficult. Talk to me," she commanded.

Ben: "You're right," he said sharply. "It is difficult. What if I can't handle the practical part of this? What if I'm really not cut out to be a physical therapist? What if this plan is a big mistake?" His voice trailed off. He looked overwhelmed and disconsolate.

Betsy: "Sure, you have second thoughts. I wonder about teaching too sometimes. I guess if either of us makes a mistake, we'll try something else. Until we are proven to be wrong, however, let's assume we are on course." Betsy's voice softened as she went on.

"No matter what you decide to do vocationally, I'll still admire you and care deeply for you. Whether you become a physical therapist or something else, I am on your side." She squeezed his hand.

Ben was thrown off track again. She said "admire and care deeply." That could border on love. It was time to nail this down.

"Could we switch topics for a few minutes?" Ben asked. He didn't wait for her response. "Let's discuss our relationship." Suddenly Ben seemed re-energized. Betsy was taken aback.

They began a discussion which continued throughout the remainder of the drive and on into the time they organized Ben's apartment. They acknowledged that they were serious about each other and reached a clear understanding about the nature and direction of the relationship. (pp. 47-48)

Because both Ben and Betsy were internally connected, they knew how they felt. With this strong internal attachment to their own feelings, they could move one step further and empathetically connect to each other's. As a couple, they could give and receive empathy and non-judgmental understanding.

In contrast, Tricia and Tom were more dissimilar. The role models in their respective parental homes had been different, so their internal connectedness and ability to be empathetic were dissimilar. In Tricia's family, emotions were unimportant. They were neither to be felt nor expressed. Conversation was about people, possessions, finances, activities, and politics. It was cognitive and factual.

However, in Tom's family, each morning his parents discussed the daily schedule. In the evening they reviewed both the activities of the day and their personal feelings about these experiences. The conversation involved both head and heart. Facts and feelings were intertwined.

When Tricia and Tom dated, Tricia, like her parents, focused on the rational, cognitive part of life. Personal and professional knowledge, competency, and success were the foci. Tricia was bright, capable, and intellectual. Tom enjoyed her broad, cosmopolitan view of life and the stimulation that it provided. The world had dramatically increased in scope. Talk about daily events and personal feelings seemed trite. Besides, Tricia saw them as irrelevant and rather provincial.

Although at this point the relationship was full of excitement, Tricia and Tom had the perfect setup for poor communication, lack of empathy, and intense conflict. Heart-to-heart conversation did not and would not happen.

Tricia was not internally connected to her feelings. Consequently, she was unable to label and express them directly to Tom, a situation which made empathy between them impossible. Her migraine headache after church is a good example of how indirectly she felt and worked through her feelings. Because she was not clearly aware of her emotions, she could not share them directly with Tom. Empathy between them was disallowed.

Since she was not directly connected to her feelings, she simply reacted when they overwhelmed her. She either responded physically via a symptom like a migraine headache, or verbally through sarcasm and cutting comments. Rather than Tricia being able to identify her emotions and handle them constructively, they built up and overwhelmed her. The skiing scenario illustrates the problem:

> After several attempts, she became frustrated. With intense disgust, she quit. As she got into the boat, she was furious.

Tricia: "What a ridiculous sport. Who would want to do this, anyway? Bimbos, I guess. Forget it. Is this your idea of a joke?" Tricia asked.

Tom: "Sometimes it can take a little time to learn. You looked particularly good on the second and third tries. I know you feel discouraged. I did too when I learned. You certainly gave it your best shot," Tom said empathetically.

Tricia: "This is a ridiculous sport. I won't try it again. I hope your other ideas aren't as bad as this one," Tricia said with blame and sarcasm in her voice.

> Her comments stung, but Tom tried to shrug them off. After all, it had been a long trip and she was probably tired. Besides, people probably didn't water ski in Washington, D.C. Perhaps it really was a bad idea.

> Although Tom enjoyed the sport himself, he didn't ask Tricia to drive the boat so he could ski. He didn't want to flaunt his expertise. Instead, they did a little more sightseeing on the lake and then put the boat back on the trailer and returned home. (p. 43)

Although Tom initially responded empathetically, he quickly backed off and swallowed his feelings. As the relationship progresses, there is a high probability that he will either withdraw and keep quiet as he did during the skiing fiasco or strike back. Either response precludes empathy and creates increased conflict and distance. Although Tom has the ability both to be internally connected and to give and receive empathy, it will be consistently disallowed in this relationship.

Whereas Betsy and Ben each have internal connectedness and the capacity for mutual empathy, Tricia and Tom struggle. Tricia simply reacts to her feelings. She experiences physical symptoms or becomes sarcastic. Without internal connectedness, empathy between them will not occur. Shared values and empathy are absent in their relationship.

CHAPTER 3

ASSERTIVENESS

W hen Tricia lashed out at Tom after she tried to water ski, he quickly backed off and became quiet. The interchange demonstrated not only the lack of her internal connectedness and hence their inability to share empathy, but also the challenge they face on how to deal with anger constructively.

ANGER

As background to our discussion on anger, it is helpful to consider the frequently held misconception that some feelings are positive and others are negative. The following chart illustrates those that might fall into each of these categories.

Concept of Positive and
Negative Feelings

BAD/NEGATIVE	GOOD/POSITIVE
Anger	Love
Frustration	Concern
Fear	Joy
Anxiety	Happiness
Hurt	Enthusiasm
Disappointment	Gratitude
Disgust	Sympathy
Grief	Warmth

In reality, feelings are neither good nor bad, neither positive nor negative. They simply are. They all will be experienced at some point over the course of a lifetime. The issue is not whether specific emotions should be felt but rather how they can be appropriately processed and expressed. To feel angry from time to time is inevitable. But if anger is handled destructively, empathy and emotional intimacy will be disallowed. Psychological distance will occur. If processed constructively, the opposite will happen. Anger expressed in a positive manner can actually increase intimacy.

In accordance with the theory that some feelings are positive and some are negative, it is assumed that only the positive ones are to be felt and expressed. The others are not to be experienced, but if they are, they are definitely not to be stated. The assumption is that if negative emotions are felt and, even worse, if they are shared, they can only be destructive. If they are expressed, they will wreak havoc. Therefore, if they are experienced, it is preferable to bottle them up and keep them inside. Eventually, according to the theory, they will disappear.

BOTTLING UP

In reality, if feelings are bottled up, they do not disappear. Instead they come out in indirect ways. Let's say your spouse has been late for dinner four consecutive nights. The family has faithfully waited to eat, although the children have gotten cranky and the meals have been overcooked. On the fifth evening, your spouse agrees to bring home a gallon of milk and a loaf of bread, both of which are needed for the meal. Your mate walks in at the designated time but without the milk and bread. Until now you have said nothing about the frustration related to the four late dinners, but this is the last straw.

You angrily reprimand your mate for being inconsiderate, thoughtless, and self-centered, and you do this with great vehemence. "I can't believe you forgot the milk and bread. Here we are waiting for you and the staples, and you forgot. Forgot! How self-focused can you be? Do your wife and children mean anything to you? How can you be so thoughtless and inconsiderate? What kind of husband and father are you?"

From your partner's perspective, your anger is disproportionate to the offense related to the milk and bread. He doesn't understand that you released the pent-up anger and resentment that you had accumulated over the week. The feelings about four late dinners were added to those about the forgotten milk and bread. The result was intense anger. You popped your top, emptied your bottle of anger, and now you feel relieved. In contrast, your spouse is stunned and surprised that forgetting the milk and bread could cause such a furor. Your partner does not realize that over the week you have filled your bottle with anger, and now, with this explosion, you have emptied it.

If you have bottled-up anger, you too may find that one last hurt is the straw that breaks the camel's back. You explode and when you do, your anger is disproportionate to the offense. You pop your top, empty all of the anger you have saved, and feel relieved. However, the person on the receiving end reels from the experience. Your reaction has been much more intense than expected.

In addition to popping your top, there are several other reactions related to bottled-up anger. You may have physical symptoms. Like Tricia, you may have headaches. Or, you may experience back problems, diarrhea, high blood pressure, or heart palpitations. You may turn your anger inward and become depressed, eat too much or too little, smoke, drink, or use drugs.

You may express your anger by being sexually unfaithful. In respect to sexual unfaithfulness, we will discuss the devastation of infidelity in Chapter 7. Unfaithfulness presents a set of challenges to a relationship like no other. Hence, Chapter 8 deals exclusively with the issue of forgiveness.

Like Tricia, you may express your anger via sarcasm and cutting comments. Although this method may be tempting, it is highly destructive. To illustrate, imagine that week after week your partner has promised that soon you will spend a weekend away together. Months pass. More important things continually supersede the anticipated weekend retreat. You say nothing, but the anger builds.

When you are out with other couples and they talk about their recent get-away weekends or vacations, you make comments like, "Some people are married to Santa Claus and others are married to Scrooge." Or, "I am married to Pinocchio. See the long nose? Lots of lies and broken promises."

You do not deal with the issue directly and privately but rather indirectly, publicly, and hurtfully. The point is made with sarcasm and cutting comments. Your spouse is openly chastised and embarrassed. Over time, this method of handling anger chips away at the relationship.

Along with sarcasm and cutting comments, passive-aggressive behavior is an all-too-frequent method used to handle anger. You aggressively get back at your spouse but in a passive manner—hence the term "passive-aggressive."

Using the same example of the broken promises about the weekend away, the offended spouse would deal with the related anger by intentionally forgetting to pick up the dry cleaning required for the next business trip or by being too tired for any sexual involvement. In a passive yet quietly aggressive manner, the offended partner punishes the offender. The anger about the broken promises is subtly and hurtfully expressed.

AGGRESSIVENESS

In contrast to the bottling-up approach, which includes all of the above-noted behaviors, there is another common method to handle anger, namely, aggressiveness. With aggressiveness, anger is expressed directly and destructively. In regard to the weekend retreat, the emotions are stated forcefully and in a hostile, accusatory manner.

"You are disgusting. You always make promises that you never keep. We are never going to have a weekend away. You are a fake and a liar."

Absolutes like "always" and "never" are coupled with accusations and "you" messages. The verbal attack can escalate into emotional, physical, or sexual abuse. Bottled-up anger is destructive to a relationship, but so too is aggressive anger. It can intensify to the point of violence and become life-threatening. If this type of destructive interaction occurs, it strikes at the core of the relationship. The marriage is unsafe emotionally and perhaps physically and sexually as well.

The diagram that follows illustrates these two common ways to handle anger, namely, bottling-up and aggressiveness.

Two Common Ways to Handle Anger

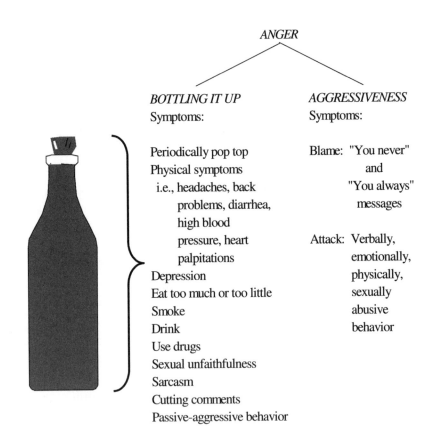

ANGER

BOTTLING IT UP
Symptoms:

Periodically pop top
Physical symptoms
  i.e., headaches, back
    problems, diarrhea,
    high blood
    pressure, heart
    palpitations
Depression
Eat too much or too little
Smoke
Drink
Use drugs
Sexual unfaithfulness
Sarcasm
Cutting comments
Passive-aggressive behavior

AGGRESSIVENESS
Symptoms:

Blame: "You never"
      and
    "You always"
     messages

Attack: Verbally,
    emotionally,
    physically,
    sexually
    abusive
    behavior

ASSERTIVENESS

Happily, there is a third way to handle anger. It is called assertiveness, and it is crucial to the design of a successful relationship. It is a method that facilitates empathy and increased intimacy.

Assertiveness requires internal problem-solving as discussed in the previous chapter and diagrammed on page 52. The process would begin with head and heart being internally connected. In the example of the promised get-away weekend which consistently does not occur, the internal connectedness could be diagrammed as follows.

Internal Connectedness and Assertiveness

1) FACTS
- I know my spouse is busy. The company is growing rapidly and the demands on him are intense. I should be patient.

2) FEELINGS
- I am furious. Week after week the promised retreat does not occur.

This internal connectedness is a prerequisite for problem-solving. Your head and heart respectively need to state the specific facts you are considering and emotions you are feeling. Once clarity about each is gained, you can move into the problem-solving mode and develop alternatives—which include bottling-up, aggressiveness, and assertiveness. Then you can make a decision and take action.

If your decision is to be assertive, you can share the feelings and reasons for them via the sentence stem,

I feel _____ because _____.
         (feelings)   (reasons)

For example, I feel angry because our weekends away don't materialize. It seems that other things are more important than our relationship.

After you assertively share your anger about the weekend retreats which do not materialize, your mate can better understand your emotional pain and struggle. However, the weekend away may or may not occur in the future. If it does, it is a fringe benefit. Resolution may or may not happen, but understanding will.

The following diagram summarizes the entire process of internal problem-solving which makes it possible to be assertive.

Internal Problem-Solving
Related to Assertiveness

1)   FACTS
- I know my spouse is busy. The company is growing rapidly and the demands on him are intense. I should be patient.

2)   FEELINGS
- I am furious. Week after week the promised retreat does not occur.

3)    DEVELOP OPTIONS
- Bottle up anger
- Aggressiveness
- Assertiveness

MAKE A DECISION
- Be assertive

TAKE ACTION
- I feel angry because our weekends away don't materialize.
- I feel angry because it seems that other things are more important than our relationship.*

---

* The purpose of assertiveness is to handle feelings constructively. Resolution may or may not occur.

Let's use the example about the late dinners and the forgotten milk and bread to demonstrate again the process of assertiveness. After going through the internal problem-solving related to assertiveness, the presentation would sound as follows. "I feel angry because of how this week has developed. For four nights I have waited to serve dinner even though the children were cranky and the meal was overcooked, and now we have no milk and bread for this meal. I feel hurt and angry because my needs and the family's needs seem secondary to yours."

As already noted, resolution is a fringe benefit. You may or may not eat after 8:00 p.m. in the future. Your spouse might or might not forget the milk and bread again. However, your anger has been constructively expressed. Your mate knows how you feel and can try to honor your needs and desires. With assertiveness, you can release the pressure without an explosion and provide a forum in which understanding, and perhaps resolution, can occur. In a marriage relationship, both partners need to have the skill of assertiveness. With this skill, anger can be handled constructively.

As an aside, if you try to be assertive and your spouse becomes defensive, review what you have said. Perhaps inadvertently you used the words "you always" or "you never." If so, ask your spouse if you may begin the conversation again. Make the dialogue as constructive as possible.

In summary then, you can handle anger in three ways: bottle it up, be aggressive, or use assertiveness. The diagram that follows summarizes these alternatives. As illustrated in this chapter, the third option is a required component for a mutually supportive marriage relationship.

Three Options with Anger

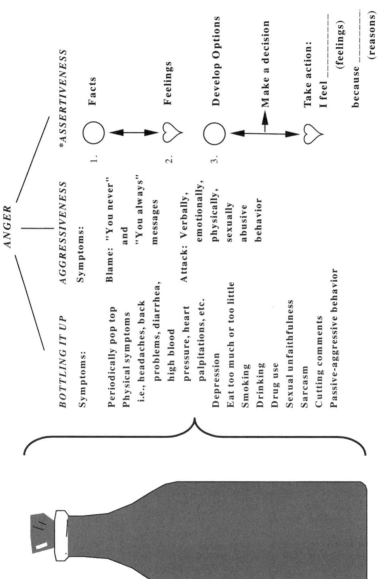

ANGER

BOTTLING IT UP	*AGGRESSIVENESS*	*ASSERTIVENESS*
Symptoms:	Symptoms:	

BOTTLING IT UP

Symptoms:

Periodically pop top
Physical symptoms
i.e., headaches, back
problems, diarrhea,
high blood
pressure, heart
palpitations, etc.
Depression
Eat too much or too little
Smoking
Drinking
Drug use
Sexual unfaithfulness
Sarcasm
Cutting comments
Passive-aggressive behavior

AGGRESSIVENESS

Symptoms:

Blame: "You never"
and
"You always"
messages

Attack: Verbally,
emotionally,
physically,
sexually
abusive
behavior

ASSERTIVENESS

1. Facts

2. Feelings

3. Develop Options

Make a decision

Take action:
I feel _____
(feelings)
because _____
(reasons)

*Resolution is a fringe benefit if it occurs.

The more intense the feelings, the more important it is to be assertive. Assertiveness can be used with all emotions, but it is especially helpful with difficult ones such as sadness, fear, anger, and hurt. To demonstrate:

- I feel sad because today is the anniversary of our child's death.
- I feel fearful when we seriously disagree because I am afraid you will leave me.
- I feel angry and hurt because your work during tax season creates a major disruption in our family life.

Assertiveness is a skill that allows all feelings to be shared in a constructive manner. When it is used, defensiveness decreases, and the potential for emotional intimacy increases. Assertiveness can transform anger and conflict into increased closeness. When difficult feelings are constructively expressed, the relationship can grow stronger over time.

RAGE

Within this discussion of anger, it is important to explore the related feeling of rage. Anger is connected to a specific offense which has happened recently. The 8:00 p.m. dinners, the forgotten milk and bread, and the weekend trips that do not materialize are current offenses. Thus, present anger is felt and addressed in an assertive manner.

In contrast, rage is anger saved over time. Rage is old anger kept in the bottle for many years. With time, more pain and anger are added. As feelings accumulate, the bottle fills. There is less and less space for any new emotions. At any time, one last feeling can overfill the bottle and an emotional explosion occurs with great force. A current offense precipitates the explosion. Rage is vented with intensity and may spiral out of control.

If you live with either your own or your partner's rage, you know it. It feels as if there is an ever-present powder keg which can explode at any moment.

Rage is usually tied to the past, often the far distant past. It may emanate from the pain of a troubled childhood. Its source may be emotional, physical, or sexual abuse. It may be the result of alcohol or drug addiction in your family. There are many reasons for rage. However, although the trauma happened in the past, the intense emotions are carried into and can greatly influence the present.

If you are the partner whose bottle is filled with rage, you may have a sense that you are edgy and easily angered. A small offense can ignite the rage. If your spouse or anyone else does something you do not like, you are suddenly filled with intense fury–much more fury than the offense would merit.

If your spouse carries the rage, you will feel as if you live with a time bomb. Any small offense, real or imagined, can ignite the short fuse. Therefore, you avoid issues. You are careful not to upset your partner and precipitate rage which could soar out of control, perhaps to the point of emotional, physical, or sexual abuse.

If rage is present, no matter how responsibly the two of you learn and practice assertiveness and the other skills discussed in this book, periodically you will have times when rage runs rampant and significant emotional damage is done to the relationship. Although you have tried to be assertive, suddenly rage will take over and escalate perhaps to the point of violence. Often the rage is precipitated by a small infraction, as the following story illustrates.

Megan and Roy live in a two-story home with their two preschool children, ages two and four. Recently, Roy began to remove his shoes when he came home each evening. He placed them on the steps leading upstairs. Since the two small children are at the age where they are determined to negotiate the stairs on their own, they often tackle the steps when Megan is busy with dinner preparation and clean-up. The shoes are a hazard. If the children trip, they could easily be injured.

Twice Megan has explained to Roy the danger related to his shoes being left on the steps, and she has done so with kindness and assertiveness. On this particular evening, she waits until the children are in bed to discuss the issue for the third time.

Megan: Roy, remember our recent discussion about your shoes? With the children up and down the stairs so often, I feel fearful because they may fall and get hurt. Would you please put your shoes either in the back hall closet or upstairs in the bedroom? I would really appreciate it.

Roy: I cannot believe you are on my back about this again. I work hard all day and you begrudge me the comfort of stocking feet. It makes me so mad. You are just like everyone else. Your needs first, first, first! (He shouts, leans forward, and pounds the arm of his chair as his voice escalates. Megan, filled with fear, instinctively recoils. Rage has taken over.)

In this example, a relatively small issue handled assertively resulted in rage. Roy's powder keg can explode at any time. Megan never knows what may set it off.

The source of the rage as well as the rage itself can be worked through in counseling. If you or your partner carry rage, it is important that you consider therapy, because no matter how dedicated you are to assertiveness and the other components discussed in this book, you will be unable to utilize them consistently until the rage is resolved. Periodically the rage will spiral out of control and destroy trust and safety in the relationship.

Whereas anger in a relationship can be expressed assertively, thereby increasing emotional intimacy and understanding, rage is destructive. If left untreated, it can create emotional distance, destroy intimacy, and perhaps become life-threatening.

With this brief consideration of rage, let's move back into our discussion of anger. How are Betsy and Ben as well as Tricia and Tom doing? What did they each have modeled in terms of how to process anger? Different families have different methods.

In Betsy's family, both her mother and father bottled it up and periodically popped their tops. Usually, the last straw would come at different times for each of them. One parent would be upset and the other would listen and say very little. After the venting, the issue died down.

On rare occasions, when both were angry simultaneously, they raised their voices and stomped around. Eventually, they talked things through.

In Ben's family, both of his parents were compassionate but strong willed. His father would periodically get very direct and aggressive. He would make accusations, draw conclusions, and issue mandates. Ben's mother would bottle up her anger and strike back in a passive-aggressive manner.

As Betsy and Ben dated, they worked through the friction points and handled anger relatively well. The trip to Madison is a good example. Initially, like his mother, Ben was rather passive-aggressive. He became sullen and wouldn't share his feelings of self-doubt and fear with Betsy. As Betsy prodded him, he snapped at her more like his father might do.

However, as Betsy's hurt and anger intensified and she probed him directly but supportively, he eventually shared his feelings. With her family experience, Betsy is not afraid of anger. She deals with her own and handles Ben's as well. Ben is tempted to be silent and passive-aggressive, but he is able to feel and discuss his feelings when he decides to do so.

As Betsy is assertive and provides a non-judgmental environment, Ben can feel safe to share his anger, fear, and other intense feelings. Although they had a somewhat tense beginning, Betsy and Ben already are using assertiveness.

Tricia and Tom were in a different situation. Tricia's parents bottled up anger as well as other emotions. Tricia's mother, like

Tricia, would get migraine headaches when she had intense feelings. Since emotions were either denied or held privately, physical symptoms were one major way to handle them. Another method was sarcasm. Her father used cutting comments to deal with his feelings.

In contrast, Tom's parents were more straightforward. Although his mother was rather long suffering, eventually she would pop her top. His father would be forthright with his anger, forthrightness which at times bordered on aggressiveness. If they both were angry simultaneously, they called it the way they saw it. They felt their emotions and expressed them verbally. After they experienced relief, they talked through the specific issue.

As has already been seen in Tricia's visit to Oshkosh, she bottled up her feelings. They came to expression only indirectly through headaches and sarcasm. She combined her mother's and father's methods of expressing anger.

If the relationship continues and the migraine headaches and cutting comments become a pattern, in all likelihood Tom will either become increasingly silent and distant or pop his top more frequently and aggressively.

As things presently stand, Tricia and Tom do not practice assertiveness. If this doesn't change, each time anger occurs it will divide rather than unify them as a couple. The emotional distance between them will increase. Over time, fewer and fewer feelings of any kind will be shared.

If a relationship is to be long term, it is mandatory to handle anger constructively. The inability of Tom and Tricia to process anger, their differences in non-negotiable values, and their inability to practice empathy are problematic. For an enduring marriage, it is necessary to have shared values, the capacity to give and receive empathy, and the ability to handle intense feelings assertively.

UNCONDITIONAL LOVE

As we follow the courtship of Betsy and Ben and Tricia and Tom, it is appropriate to discuss the topic of love. Although this could be an overwhelming assignment, it becomes manageable when love is divided into two major types: unconditional and conditional.

TWO KINDS OF LOVE

Unconditional love focuses primarily on the person and secondarily on performance. In marriage, unconditional love means you love your spouse as a person even when your mate's behavior or performance falls short of your desires and expectations. You love your spouse consistently in spite of imperfections. You accept your partner's shortcomings. Unconditional love involves continual acceptance.

In contrast, conditional love focuses primarily on performance. It becomes the measure of a person's worth. Love is given when the individual meets the necessary criteria. Thus, in marriage, the closer your spouse approximates your expectations, the more love you give. Conversely, the more your spouse falls short, the less love you give. Consciously or unconsciously, your spouse is aware of this ongoing evaluation.

With conditional love, acceptance must be constantly earned. The possibility of rejection is ever present. Conditional love requires continual attention to performance. The diagram which follows illustrates these two kinds of love.

Conditional Versus Unconditional Love

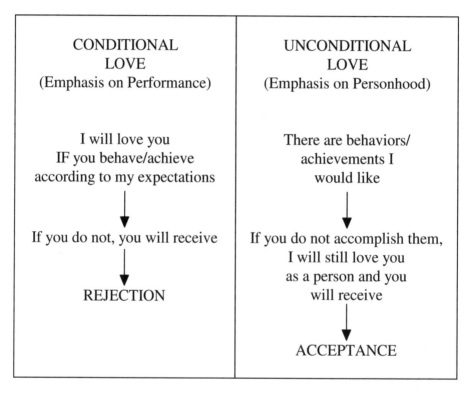

CONDITIONAL LOVE (Emphasis on Performance)	UNCONDITIONAL LOVE (Emphasis on Personhood)
I will love you IF you behave/achieve according to my expectations ↓ If you do not, you will receive ↓ REJECTION	There are behaviors/ achievements I would like ↓ If you do not accomplish them, I will still love you as a person and you will receive ↓ ACCEPTANCE

Sarah and Larry will serve to illustrate these two kinds of love. Like any couple, they have their own unique characteristics and styles. Among their differences is organizational style. With Sarah, everything has an appropriate place. With Larry, piles seem to be that appropriate place. This difference creates tension. How they resolve this issue is related to whether they love each other conditionally or unconditionally.

Sarah is very organized, almost to the point of compulsiveness. As soon as the mail arrives, she reviews it. Twice yearly, she sorts her clothes. Each weekend, she updates her list of errands as well as her progress on her short-term and long-term projects. She sends birthday and anniversary cards faithfully according to her master schedule, does her laundry and grocery shopping regularly, and completes her housework and yard work systematically.

Larry operates very differently. Mail accumulates in his study, on the dining room table, and on the kitchen counter. He is reluctant to throw anything away. In fact, he still has his elementary school keepsakes as well as his high school and college notebooks stored in boxes in the basement. No one is permitted to touch, much less sort through, any of these items. Along with his mail and old treasures, his clothes and shoes go unevaluated for years.

Imagine these two styles united in marriage. Ms. Sorter has met and married Mr. Saver. This dichotomy will serve to demonstrate the difference between conditional and unconditional love.

If Sarah loves Larry conditionally, she will frequently complain and attempt to get him to sort and organize. Whenever they are home together and the old clothes and piles of mail catch her eye, she will begin to cajole. When she sees the boxes of keepsakes that fill the basement, she will harp. Over time, her repeated nagging will severely stress the marriage.

With conditional love, the spotlight is on Larry's behavior. The focus is on the clutter and lack of organization. As Larry's behavior continues to fall short, the tension and conflict increase.

With unconditional love, this behavior is still troublesome but it is secondary to the love Sarah feels for Larry. Although she still does not appreciate Larry's behavior, she is aware that no one is perfect. She realizes and reminds herself that she would not give up the relationship for the sake of the stacks of boxes and piles of mail.

Periodically, in order to honor her own feelings, she will assertively remind Larry that she is unhappy with the clutter. She might even offer to help him sort and organize, an offer he would surely decline. Then she would let it rest. He knows how she feels and may or may not change his behavior. As previously discussed, assertiveness allows Sarah to share her feelings in a way that allows Larry to hear them. It does not guarantee that he will change his behavior.

PARENTAL TEACHING

Parents teach and model love. In all likelihood, if your parents loved you conditionally, you learned to love both yourself and others in the same way. If you have been told continually where you fall short, you probably do the same with yourself and others.

An example will serve to illustrate. If your grades were a focal point with your parents, each semester you were evaluated twice, first at school and then at home. If your grades were low, you were scolded. If they were high, you were praised.

If the primary attention and love you received revolved around academic performance, you probably concluded that your achievements are the essence of who you are. Now as an adult, you evaluate yourself on the basis of your accomplishments. Successful performance means you are acceptable; unsuccessful performance means you are unacceptable.

With unconditional love, this same scenario would be quite different. If your grades were low, your parents might have said, "We know these are difficult classes for you. We love you and want to help. Would a tutor be beneficial?" Love and respect were given to you as a person. You yourself were more important than your specific grades. Personhood was more significant than behavior. If you experienced unconditional love, you learned to allow shortcomings within yourself and in others.

Let's consider another example. Your spouse comes home and shares that the expected promotion was given to a colleague. Your mate has been passed over.

If you love your spouse conditionally, performance determines whether support is given or withheld. Your mate has fallen short. You might think and even say, "You are not as competent as your colleague. You have several major weaknesses which you have not adequately addressed. You will need to remedy those if you hope to get ahead. You should have addressed those deficiencies long before now." With this approach, which is also a good example of cross-communication and aggressiveness, your spouse will feel unsupported and unloved.

If you love your spouse unconditionally, the story would go quite differently. When your mate shared that the position was given to someone else, you might say, "You must feel very disappointed, but this will not be the only promotion available. We are doing fine on our present income. You tried and that is what counts. Next time, it may be your turn to move up the ranks." With this approach, which is also a good example of empathy, your spouse feels supported and accepted. Performance is secondary to personhood. Your spouse is loved with or without the promotion. Unconditional love is a necessary component for an enduring relationship.

How have you learned to love yourself? With an attitude of evaluation and judgment, or one of acceptance? How do you love others? Obviously, both of these impact your marriage. It is important that you love yourself and your partner unconditionally.

Love Continuum

In order to help you assess how you have been loved and how you love yourself and others including your mate, please complete the following chart. Think of love as a continuum with the maximum of conditional love at the far left and the maximum of unconditional love at the far right. For the questions that follow about your parents, yourself, and your spouse, put an X at the appropriate point on the continuum. As you do this exercise, you will gain helpful insight concerning how you were loved and have learned to love yourself and others.

Love Continuum

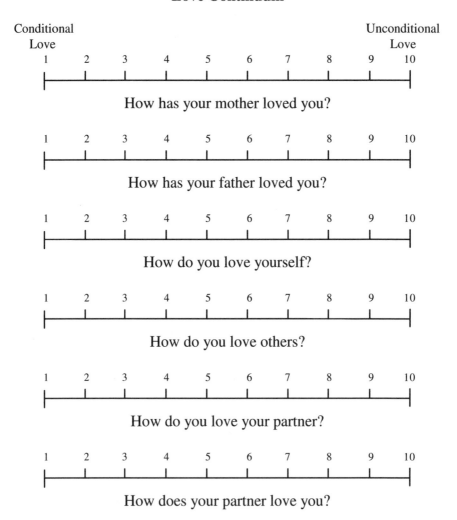

Conditional
 Love

Unconditional
 Love

1   2   3   4   5   6   7   8   9   10

How has your mother loved you?

1   2   3   4   5   6   7   8   9   10

How has your father loved you?

1   2   3   4   5   6   7   8   9   10

How do you love yourself?

1   2   3   4   5   6   7   8   9   10

How do you love others?

1   2   3   4   5   6   7   8   9   10

How do you love your partner?

1   2   3   4   5   6   7   8   9   10

How does your partner love you?

If your answers reveal that conditional rather than unconditional love permeates your life and relationships, this can be changed. If your parents loved you conditionally, via counseling you can explore and understand the family dynamics and get free of this judgmental pattern. You need not love yourself and/or your spouse in this way. Ultimately, you will find that acceptance is much less work than constant evaluation of yourself and your spouse. Unconditional love makes life easier and more free-flowing.

Unconditional love for yourself and your partner is the ideal in a marriage. However, such love does not mean you happily accept any behavior. It means you address the troublesome behaviors in the larger context of love, just as Sarah did with Larry.

From time to time, in an assertive manner, Sarah indicated how difficult it was for her to handle what she viewed as Larry's lack of organization. However, the love she and Larry shared and the worth they placed on the relationship far outweighed this annoyance. Their conflict was dealt with within the framework of their loving relationship. Love and acceptance were constants in their marriage.

How do our two couples, Betsy and Ben, Tricia and Tom, operate with regard to love? Both Betsy and Ben received unconditional love. Betsy received it very consistently from both parents.

However, because of the way Ben's father handled anger, Ben sometimes struggled to love himself and to feel internally secure. Sometimes, in anger, his father would call him up short. He would tell him where he failed, what he should change, and how he needed to accomplish that change. Although Ben was loved unconditionally for the majority of the time, when his father angrily and aggressively focused on his behavior and performance, Ben got a bit shaken and felt he was loved conditionally.

All in all, however, Betsy and Ben love themselves and each other unconditionally. Ben didn't love Betsy any less because she could not water-ski. Betsy didn't love Ben any less when he had doubts about becoming a physical therapist.

Tricia and Tom are in a different situation. Tricia is from a success-oriented family, where each member was expected to act and look perfect. Often, her father's sarcasm and cutting comments were directed at what he perceived to be her mother's shortcomings. To be imperfect meant to receive less love. For each family member, the emphasis was on behavior and performance.

Although for the most part Tricia was successful, she knew she had to toe the line. Even though she was attractive and competent, she was aware of the continuous scrutiny. Thus, she learned to love herself conditionally. She had extremely high expectations and became angry if she did not measure up. The water-skiing fiasco was a good example.

Although she demanded somewhat less of others, her expectations of those closest to her, like Tom, were very high. She chose Tom because he too was going to be a professional. She planned to mold him into the perfect spouse. What a setup for pain.

In contrast, Tom loved himself and others unconditionally. As open and free-flowing as thoughts and feelings were in his home, so too were love and acceptance. There was no room for intolerance and judgment.

If Tricia and Tom marry, Tricia will expect Tom to be more–more professional, wealthy, and cosmopolitan. With conditional love, the focus is on behavior and performance. Tom will struggle to understand and accept Tricia's expectations. However, over time, her control and coercion will erode Tom's capacity to unconditionally love himself and her.

For a long-lasting marriage, unconditional love needs to be added to the list of design requirements. Shared non-negotiable values, empathy, assertiveness, and unconditional love create a strong marital foundation. However, one more component needs to be part of the design. It is the skill of compromise.

CHAPTER 5

COMPROMISE

Although there were many significant differences between Tricia and Tom in regard to non-negotiable values and abilities related to empathy, assertiveness, and unconditional love, they decided to pursue their relationship. As Tom started veterinary school at Michigan State University, Tricia began her senior year at the University of Maryland.

As the year progressed, Tom encouraged Tricia to join a public accounting firm in Michigan after graduation. However, she was determined to remain on the East Coast. Accordingly, Tom decided to transfer at the end of his first year. However, this was discouraged by his faculty members. Tom missed Tricia and decided to discuss his feelings with her by telephone.

"Tricia, I really miss you. It's hard to concentrate. You are so far away. I feel pulled in two directions, toward school and toward you. Do you have a similar struggle?" Tom asked.

"I can't afford to have that struggle. I need to work in one of the major public accounting firms in order to earn my CPA designation. Contacts with the right clients are critical in order to become a partner. You need to focus on your goals too. Once we get our professions in order, we can think about proximity. To miss each other is a luxury we can't afford," Tricia stated emphatically.

Tom felt disheartened. He had shared his heart, and Tricia had cut him off. She had responded with her head. He felt unheard and discounted. Cross-communication had occurred. Instead of empathy and understanding, he had gotten a lesson and a directive.

From time to time, he tried again to discuss this issue, but with no success. Eventually, he adjusted. He focused less on his relationship with Tricia and more on his studies in veterinary medicine. However, he was angry. He felt unheard, unloved, and helpless to either influence Tricia or change the situation. He bottled up his feelings.

Tom and Tricia were scheduled to be together over the Christmas holidays. When Tom reached Washington, D.C., it was difficult to feign excitement. He was hurt and angry because of their many unsatisfactory discussions. When they arrived at the town house late in the evening and he realized they were alone, he popped his top and did so in a rather accusatory manner.

"I am not certain why I am here, Tricia. I am not sure we have a relationship. We have dated for nearly a year, and my needs and feelings seem to mean nothing to you. You won't seriously consider a position with an accounting firm in Michigan even though you know I can't transfer. You are focused on your CPA designation and career. Clearly, I am second or third on your priority list. How important is this relationship?"

As Tom talked, Tricia became silent and withdrawn. When Tom finished, Tricia said curtly, "I am tired and I am going to bed. We can discuss this tomorrow." And with that, she went to her room.

The next day Tricia was debilitated by a migraine headache. Although she and Tom were together in the same house, there was neither discussion nor quality time. Although Tom felt relieved because he had emptied his bottle of anger, he felt guilty about the blunt delivery. He felt compassion for the emotional and physical pain he had obviously caused Tricia.

He stayed with her and was very quiet, concerned, and helpful. Gradually, she recovered. After two days, she felt better. The issue of their relationship was not discussed.

There were several holiday parties scheduled with Tricia's friends and family, and Tom was ready. He had emotionally reconnected. He was in touch with his love for Tricia. Although she wasn't perfect, she was the most brilliant, cosmopolitan woman he had ever met. He loved her unconditionally. Once again he was charming, humorous, and attentive.

However, Tricia was disgruntled that Tom was back to normal. How could he treat her so harshly and then pretend everything was fine? She was furious. His behavior chipped away at her love and patience. She expected better of him. He definitely fell short, and she found him less attractive. She had mixed feelings about being with him. She felt he needed to be brought down a peg.

While at a party with friends, the anger welled up. She observed him as he stood near the hors d'oeuvre table surrounded by her friends who had grown very fond of him. They laughed as he told a story, probably some funny or endearing animal story.

She walked over and said sarcastically, "Is Dr. Doolittle jocular and entertaining? Perhaps he missed his calling. He should be a stand-up comedian."

Embarrassed silence fell on the group. Then someone made a comment to divert the conversation. The evening went on. Now that his intense anger was gone, Tom was able to exercise patience. He let her put-down pass. Tricia made a few other cutting comments over the course of the evening, and then her anger too began to dissolve.

She thought little about her sarcasm. After all, it was how her father called her mother up short when she had gotten out of line. Tricia knew how she expected to be treated, and Tom had better get his marching orders straight if he expected her love. She would love him if he behaved appropriately.

After both had dissipated their anger, they emotionally reconnected. By the end of the holiday season, they decided to become engaged after Tricia's graduation in the spring.

While Tricia and Tom were experiencing tension and disagreement about where Tricia would locate geographically, Betsy and Ben shared a common goal. They wanted to be together as soon as possible. Ben encouraged Betsy to find a teaching position somewhere in Wisconsin, preferably in the greater Madison area.

She was open to the idea. To be close to Ben was more important than to live on the East Coast.

They talked often on the phone about Ben's academic and professional challenges as well as Betsy's student teaching and job search. One evening when Ben had had a particularly difficult time with his supervisor, Jim, and needed to talk about his frustration, he called her and explained the situation and feelings.

"Dr. Wagner came down on us in team meeting today. He was very upset about how disjointedly we had handled the new admission. He ranted and raved and then the meeting ended. Afterwards, my supervisor, Jim, leaned on me as though I was somehow in charge. I am not in charge. I didn't get assigned to the case until three full days after the admission and I have played catch-up ever since. I have worked diligently and responsibly to better understand the patient's medical situation so I can develop the appropriate physical therapy treatment plan. Jim continues to blame me. I know I am long-suffering, but I have just about had it with him. Sometimes patience is not a virtue."

Betsy listened supportively and responded empathetically. "He certainly is being difficult–a real pain. He just doesn't see what a competent, conscientious person you are. He will realize it with time. I wish I were there with you. I'd take you out for a pepperoni pizza. That would fix everything." They both laughed. Ben's tension disappeared.

"When we talk, it makes me doubly eager to have you live closer. I'll be near my best friend, you. I love you, Betsy."

"I love you too. It will be wonderful when we can be together more often."

"Too good to be true. Keep me posted on your job search. I'll evaluate the shortest route from Madison to each city in which you interview. As I look forward to the future, I realize that this too shall pass. Jim is only a temporary problem. I know life is never going to be perfect, but I am ready to move on."

Like Tom and Tricia, Ben and Betsy had made plans to be together over the Christmas break. Betsy flew to Oshkosh. They both felt her visit was perfectly timed because a paternal intergenerational family reunion was scheduled. Betsy knew Ben would proudly introduce her to all of his relatives and explain to her in a quiet voice the various family relationships.

However, after she arrived in Oshkosh, he told her he wouldn't be at the reunion because he had to work. Betsy was angry and disappointed. Her temper flared.

"Are you telling me I came all the way out here to meet your extended family, and now I have to do it without you? This is a real rip-off. You mean you couldn't get your work schedule changed?"

"No, I couldn't. Don't be on my case about it. I told you Jim is a bear. How do you think I feel?"

That question stopped Betsy in her tracks. He too must be very angry and disappointed. Betsy became silent and after a few moments of deliberation softly said, "I guess I am more disappointed than angry. I'm sorry I lost my temper. I am a big girl and can adjust." Betsy grabbed his hand and said with a twinkle in her eye, "I'll miss you, but your dad will be next best to having you. Actually, your dad is pretty stiff competition, you know." She giggled, and Ben laughed with relief.

"I'm disappointed too. We get so little time together, and Jim has no appreciation of that."

"Or anything else for that matter. Oh, well, it could be worse. Let's adjust and move on. I am just glad we are together. I have missed you tremendously," she said as she kissed him lovingly.

Again the difference between the two couples is apparent. When Tom attempted to bring up and resolve emotional issues either on the telephone or face to face, Tricia exercised cross-communication, had a migraine headache, or retaliated with sarcasm and cutting comments. Issues and emotions were left unsettled.

In contrast, Ben and Betsy dealt with their emotions straightforwardly. Although they initially expressed their feelings rather aggressively, they quickly became assertive and moved toward resolution. The holiday visit went well.

In the spring, Betsy got a teaching position in a suburban Madison school. She and Ben would be only forty-five minutes apart. In the fall, she moved into an apartment with another single teacher. Soon thereafter, she and Ben became engaged. Life was rich and full of promise.

As Betsy started her teaching job in the Madison area, Tricia assumed her position with the public accounting firm of Van, Lee, & Smith in Washington, D.C. She was thrilled. Her parents' connections had paved the way.

Hundreds of miles separated Tricia and Tom, but Tricia would have it no other way. This was her choice. She was determined to attain her CPA designation and move toward partnership. Consequently, their engagement was long and rocky.

However, when they were together, once they had expressed the bottled-up anger, they thoroughly enjoyed each other's company. When things were not stressed, they had great fun.

Tricia became a CPA and stayed at the firm while Tom finished veterinary school. During that time, they began to discuss the issue of where geographically they would settle when they married.

By this time, Ben and Betsy were married and had already resolved the matter of initial location. The method by which each couple reached their decision will be discussed later in this chapter.

In a relationship, joint decision-making is a critical skill. In order to make the variety of required decisions, couples need to have a workable, systematic process.

DECISION-MAKING

In a marriage, decisions generally are made in one of three ways. Partners may take turns. For example, if you planned the last vacation and you both did what you preferred, your spouse gets to plan the next one, and you will do what your partner enjoys. The emphasis is on equality. This method often results in mates keeping score. Each is entitled to make the same number of important decisions. Therefore, they both keep tally.

Or, spouses may divide up and designate who will make which decisions. For example, you make the decisions on the type and model of car, the location of the house, and which school the children will attend. Your partner decides what particular appliance will be purchased, how often as a couple you will entertain, and which church you will attend. Whereas the first method involves taking turns, the second is a division of labor. Each mate is assigned specific decisions.

Or, a couple may do what is called positional bargaining. Each of you takes a position, develops the rationale to support this specific view, and then tries to convince the other to swing to that perspective. An example will serve to illustrate.

You decide you want to move into a larger house in a different neighborhood. You come up with reasons why this move is appropriate and necessary. The children need their own rooms, a recreation room in which to play, and a school system with more enrichment programs. Since your spouse does not want to move, your partner takes the opposite position and develops a list of reasons why you as a family should remain in your present home: the house payments are manageable, the children have roots, they have done fine with shared bedrooms and use of the playroom, and to change schools would be traumatic.

With positional bargaining each of you takes a position, lists your reasons, and works to convince the other to think as you do. This method is like a debate contest, and, as with such a contest, there is a winner and a loser. However, in a marriage relationship, to win is bittersweet. If you prevail and your partner is unhappy, it will be difficult to enjoy your victory. The reverse is also true. Therefore, no matter who wins, the relationship loses.

Whether you move or stay in your present home is really secondary. Love is strained. Positional bargaining divides rather than unifies you as spouses and results in at least one of you feeling hurt, disappointed, and angry. No matter who wins, the relationship suffers.

LOVE AND COMPROMISE

In addition to these three common ways to make decisions within a marriage, there is a fourth, which is compromise. This skill is pivotal to a long-term relationship. To understand how compromise works, it is helpful to appreciate the nature of the love on which it is built. Therefore, within the broad framework of unconditional love, let's discuss the specific expression of love required for compromise.

This type of love involves each spouse valuing the other's wants and needs equally as much as his or her own. Neither tries to win, but both seek to find a mutually satisfying resolution. They want a win/win decision that honors the wants and needs of both of them.

Compromise means that, although you as a couple begin with divergent views or preferences, you talk through these differences to the point where you are able to reach a mutually rewarding solution. Rather than keep score, divide the decisions, or do positional bargaining, you together reach a win/win decision where both of you are pleased with the outcome.

PROCESS OF COMPROMISE

Compromise requires teamwork and produces a sense of partnership. It is a three-step process in which: (1) each spouse's wants and needs are expressed, (2) options related to these wants and needs are developed, (3) and a mutually satisfactory decision among these options is made. This is a method of creative problem-solving between mates wherein a win/win as opposed to a win/lose resolution is reached. Let's explore the process in greater detail.

First, you together list your wants and needs. These are taken at face value. They are simply accepted and recorded. There is no pressure to change them. When this is completed, your mutual goal is to fulfill this list of wants and needs.

During step one, you are cooperative. You function as partners. All of the wants and needs on the list, no matter which of you states them, are equally important to both of you. Love is happening. Love is when your spouse's wants and needs are equally important to you as your own.

Second, based on this list of wants and needs, you together develop as many options as possible. All ideas, no matter how far-fetched, are listed because often the ultimate decision involves a combination of the various alternatives. As you brainstorm, you will see that there are many more options than the original two you had with positional bargaining.

Third, after the two of you have explored and considered each of the alternatives you have listed, you reach a mutually satisfying decision. This resolution must be win/win. If either of you is dissatisfied, you must redo the entire process until you reach a win/win decision. Both of you must be happy. The following diagram outlines the process.

Process of Compromise

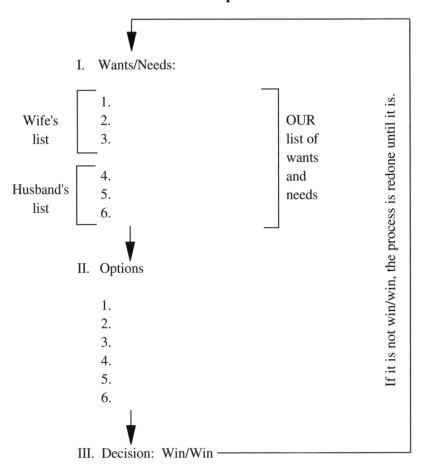

Let's use an example to fill in the diagram and illustrate the process. Barb and Peter wish to refurnish the country kitchen in their home. Peter prefers dark wood furniture, and Barb likes white rattan.

If they do positional bargaining, their respective positions are clear. They have two options, dark wood or white rattan. Each would gather reasons and attempt to swing the other over to his or her perspective. In all probability, one of them would eventually win and the other would lose. However, no matter who won and who lost, the relationship would suffer.

In contrast, with compromise, the three-step process would unfold as diagrammed on page 102. Both would list their wants and needs as related to the furniture. Peter states he wants the room to be cozy. He desires the furniture in it to both wear well and include wall units with bookshelves. Barb, in turn, indicates that she would like the room to have an open and airy look and feel. She prefers to decorate with painted pastel furniture rather than wood grains. She too wants bookshelves in this room.

Already in step one something very important has occurred. Instead of the two of them being entrenched in their respective positions of dark wood and white rattan, they have developed a shared list of desires. They record each other's wants and needs and exert no pressure to alter them. They are open-minded and cooperative. The list that results establishes the goals they wish to attain.

Based on this list, they develop options. They can consider not only dark wood and white rattan, but also various other pastel colors of rattan as well as light and dark wood tones. Further, they can add Danish modern to the list. This style would be wood but with a more open look. Whereas they originally had only two alternatives, they now have several. They work as a team to generate as many ideas as possible.

After Barb and Peter have shopped, evaluated, and discussed enough, they can make a decision. However, the decision must be win/win. If both of them are not pleased, they must redo the process. They need to do it until they truly have arrived at a mutually satisfying resolution. This process operationalizes the definition of love wherein each spouse's wants and needs are equally important.

Eventually, Barb and Peter decided on light woodtone rattan. Their process can be diagrammed as follows.

Completed Process of Compromise

I. Wants/Needs:

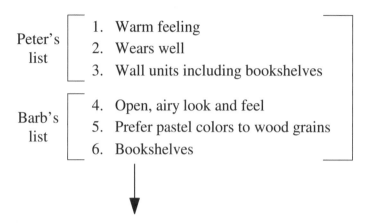

Peter's list
1. Warm feeling
2. Wears well
3. Wall units including bookshelves

Barb's list
4. Open, airy look and feel
5. Prefer pastel colors to wood grains
6. Bookshelves

Peter and Barb's shared list of wants and needs which become their goals

II. Options:

1. Dark wood
2. White rattan
3. Other colors of rattan
4. Light and dark woodtone rattan
5. Danish modern

III. Decision: Win/Win

Light woodtone rattan

Each time Barb and Peter or you and your spouse use this method, your confidence in each other and in your shared ability to practice love and partnership increases. No matter how different your views or desires are at the point of beginning, you can trust that, with time and compromise, you can reach a win/win resolution. This process is part of the design for a successful relationship.

If you wish to more fully understand this concept, the book entitled *Getting To Yes,* by Roger Fisher and William Ury, will prove helpful. The authors were integrally involved in the Begin/Sadat peace agreement made during President Carter's term of office. If Begin and Sadat could reach a win/win resolution after decades of dissension between Israel and Egypt, so can you.

It should be noted that the process of compromise incorporates the skills of assertiveness and empathy. The first step related to wants and needs requires both of these skills: assertiveness to share your wants and needs, and empathy to hear and accept your spouse's. You do not argue with each other about what is put on this list. Whatever each of you may want and need is simply recorded and accepted.

Issues that initially may seem impossible to resolve can actually become a means to express love and partnership, love and partnership wherein your spouse's wants and needs are equally important to you as your own. Differences can be worked out in a manner that expresses love. The bond between partners can be strengthened. When the skill of compromise is used to make decisions, love is enhanced. The probability of a long-term relationship is increased.

Since Betsy and Ben as well as Tricia and Tom needed to make a decision about geographic location, let's see how compromise worked for both couples. As already noted, the decision was more straightforward for Betsy and Ben than for Tricia and Tom. The non-negotiable values that are relevant to this decision are similar for Betsy and Ben, but dissimilar for Tricia and Tom.

Betsy and Ben treasured family time and shared activities with both parental families. They wanted a dynamic community in which to live and work so they could enjoy a comfortable lifestyle and professional fulfillment. If we lay out Betsy and Ben's process of compromise related to geographic location, it might look like this.

Betsy and Ben's Process of Compromise

I. Wants/Needs:

Betsy's list
   To be:
1. close enough to my parents to participate in family celebrations since my family gets together often.
2. close enough to spend weekend time on my parents' sailboat.
3. within driving distance of both sets of parents so that if we have children the grandparents are easily accessible.
4. in a medium size town with a progressive school system both for my sake as a teacher and our children's sake as students.

Ben's list
   To be:
5. close enough to both sets of parents that vacation time can be spent with them.
6. within driving distance of both sets of parents but perhaps closer to your family than mine because your family gets together more often.
7. far enough away that we have a sense of unity with each other and independence from both families.
8. in a town with present and future professional opportunities for both of us.

II. Options:

1. Fort Wayne or Muncie, Indiana.
2. Akron or Toledo, Ohio.
3. Harrisburg, Lancaster, or York, Pennsylvania.

III. Decision: Win/Win

Lancaster, Pennsylvania.

After Betsy and Ben sent out their respective resumes to the above-noted cities that met their shared list of wants and needs, they received three job offers that placed them both in the same city: Muncie, Toledo, and Lancaster. They explored all three, talked through the pros and cons of each, and mutually decided on Lancaster, Pennsylvania, which was approximately three hours from

Betsy's parental family and nine hours from Ben's. It was a win/win decision for both of them. Their respective needs were equally considered. Thus, when Betsy and Ben married, they moved from Madison to Lancaster. It was a win/win decision. They could establish a comfortable and fulfilling lifestyle, personally and professionally.

As alluded to in Chapter 1, Tricia and Tom have a significant challenge in connection with geographic location because this decision is integrally related to their respective non-negotiable values about their professional practices. Tricia wishes to become a partner in a high-profile public accounting firm in a major city, preferably on the East Coast. Tom wishes to do a large-animal practice in an agrarian environment.

The temptation would be for Tricia and Tom to do positional bargaining. Tricia might try to persuade Tom that a small-animal practice in a metropolitan area would be lucrative and rewarding. Tom would attempt to convince Tricia that most public accounting firms do excellent work and that the quality of the service is more important than the profile of the firm. This positional bargaining approach would cause increased friction and make the topic of geographic location even more difficult to discuss and resolve.

Even if Tricia and Tom use the process of compromise, it does not change the fact that one or both must negotiate non-negotiable values. Where they live is integral to their professional practices and to the related non-negotiable values.

They attempted to compromise. After much discussion, Tricia and Tom made a decision, recognizing it was not perfect for either of them. The process developed as follows.

Tricia and Tom's Process of Compromise

I. Wants/Needs:

Tricia's list
    To:
1. practice with a firm which minimally has a prominent regional reputation but ideally a national and international reputation.
2. live in a large metropolitan area in order to make the right personal and professional connections.
3. earn a significant income and have a cultured lifestyle.

Tom's list
    To:
4. do a large-animal practice.
5. live in a community where large animals are integral to farm life.
6. earn a fair and reasonable income; the work is more important than the money itself.

II. Options:

1. Des Moines, Iowa.
2. Minneapolis, Minnesota.
3. Madison, Wisconsin.
4. Detroit, Michigan.
5. Washington, D.C.
6. New York City.

III. Decision: Win/Win(?)

Detroit, Michigan.

Detroit is the option Tricia and Tom chose. Since Tom had attended veterinary medicine school in Michigan, he had gotten to know the geographic area. Several prestigious Eastern public accounting firms had branch offices in Detroit, plus Detroit was closer to Washington, D.C., than any of the Midwestern cities under consideration. Tricia would be able to transfer to the Van, Lee, & Smith office in Detroit and commute to Washington, D.C., one week per month and whenever else it was necessary. She and Tom could live relatively close to the city. She could travel into the metropolitan area while Tom drove into the country to do his large-animal practice.

They both realized that no matter where they settled, one or both would sacrifice. If they lived in a city Tricia selected, Tom would probably need to do a combined or perhaps exclusively small-animal practice. Clearly, he would give up the agrarian lifestyle and large-animal practice. If they selected a major city surrounded by a rural area, Tricia could practice with a large public accounting firm but not in the location she desired. This, in fact, was the decision they made.

Although there was no perfect solution, with the process of compromise they at least were clear about the respective adjustments they made for the sake of the relationship. It may work to sacrifice if it feels fair to both parties. If Tricia and Tom know they have given up something for the sake of the relationship and each feels adequately comfortable with that sacrifice, the decision could be acceptable. However, if at the onset or over time it does not feel fair, the relationship will suffer.

When a couple shares the same non-negotiable values, as with Betsy and Ben, the process can more easily result in a win/win resolution. However, with conflicting non-negotiable values, as with Tricia and Tom, there is a greater challenge. The more integral the non-negotiable value is to one's sense of self–and that is the very nature of non-negotiable values–the more difficult the process of compromise. Time will tell whether or not Tricia and Tom can live with their decision. This plan may require Tricia to stretch too far.

Before this chapter on compromise concludes, it should be noted that each time you as a couple successfully complete the process of compromise, you will realize that better decisions actually can be made when you work together as a team rather than take turns, divide decisions, or do positional bargaining. Two hearts and two heads truly are better than one. Each time you successfully complete the process, you will have put into practice the definition of love wherein your spouse's needs are equally important to you as your own. This is the last major component for designing a life-long relationship. Built on shared non-negotiable values, empathy, assertiveness, unconditional love, and the ability to compromise, your marriage can be strong and enduring.

CHAPTER 6

RELATIONSHIP EVALUATION

As the years went by, Betsy and Ben had two sons. Lancaster proved to be an ideal place to raise the boys. It had good schools and a strong sense of community. Geographically, it was close enough to share summer weekends with Betsy's parents on the boat, yet distant enough for them to lead their own family life. Ben's parents enjoyed the area and often came to visit. Betsy and Ben lived a life congruent with their values.

Within their marriage, they continued to communicate with empathy and assertiveness, love each other and the boys unconditionally, and compromise well. Their relationship was strong and emotionally intimate.

Tricia and Tom also had two children, a son and a daughter. Although Rochester Hills near Detroit was a good place for the children to live and for Tom to work, Tricia was disappointed in her professional life. Her dreams did not come true to the degree she had anticipated. Detroit would never be Washington, D.C.

Although she was a partner at Van, Lee, & Smith and simply worked out of the Detroit office, it was not the same. Even though she was in Washington, D.C., one week every month, it was not adequate. Life was different in the Midwest.

However, she was in too deeply now. The children were involved and integrated into the community. Tom had his large-animal practice. He had made his dream come true. The three of them were fulfilled. She was the only one less than happy. As was her custom, she kept quiet, had periodic migraine headaches, and from time to time was sarcastic to Tom.

Since Tricia was not attaining her professional goals, she was not particularly interested to hear about either Tom's successes or struggles. She was no more interested in his feelings than she had been when he was in veterinary school. He was the children's father and they adored him, so she felt stuck and dead-ended. Her love had faded, but she realized it was important to keep the marriage intact for the children's sake.

Heart-to-heart communication, which had always been minimal, was now non-existent. Feelings were not shared; issues were not discussed. Tricia and Tom increasingly led separate lives except for shared parenting and family time together every Saturday night. Tom and Tricia had become roommates who simply had two children in common.

RELATIONSHIP EVALUATION FORM

Based on the components discussed in this book, namely, shared non-negotiable values, empathy, assertiveness, unconditional love, and compromise, an inventory has been developed to help you and your partner evaluate the strengths and weaknesses of your relationship. This inventory is call the Relationship Evaluation Form.

The Relationship Evaluation Form has a continuum for each of the five components: non-negotiable values, empathy, assertiveness, unconditional love, and compromise. You can evaluate how you and your spouse are doing as a couple in each of these areas. The continuum ranges from 1 to 10, with 1 being low and 10 being high. Each of you can complete the form to assess the strengths and weaknesses of your relationship.

Read the directions carefully. The first four items involve a joint or team score for you and your spouse. The last item requires two individual scores, one for you and the other for your mate.

Relationship Evaluation Form

Please consider yourself and your partner as a couple on items 1 through 4. The number you select is a team score.

On the last two items, 5a and 5b, which are related to conditional and unconditional love, score yourself and your partner individually.

For every item, 1 is low and 10 is high.

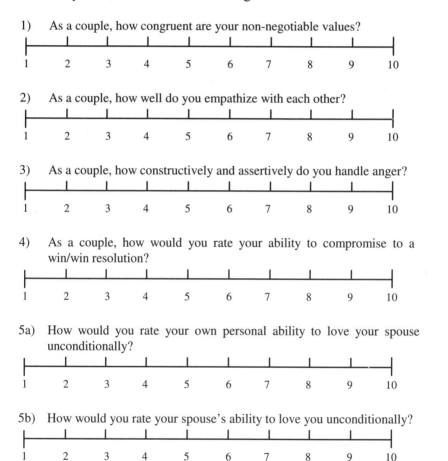

1) As a couple, how congruent are your non-negotiable values?

```
1    2    3    4    5    6    7    8    9    10
```

2) As a couple, how well do you empathize with each other?

```
1    2    3    4    5    6    7    8    9    10
```

3) As a couple, how constructively and assertively do you handle anger?

```
1    2    3    4    5    6    7    8    9    10
```

4) As a couple, how would you rate your ability to compromise to a win/win resolution?

```
1    2    3    4    5    6    7    8    9    10
```

5a) How would you rate your own personal ability to love your spouse unconditionally?

```
1    2    3    4    5    6    7    8    9    10
```

5b) How would you rate your spouse's ability to love you unconditionally?

```
1    2    3    4    5    6    7    8    9    10
```

Let's review the results of your evaluation. Consider that any dimension on which you scored six or above is in the good to excellent range, depending on the number. The higher the number, the better the congruence or level of proficiency.

If you as a couple have non-negotiable values that mesh and skills that allow you to listen to each other with empathy, share and process feelings with assertiveness, love each other unconditionally, and compromise to a win/win resolution, you have a relationship that truly can last in a vigorous way over the course of a lifetime. Your marriage is well designed.

Consider that any dimension on which you scored five or below needs improvement. If you scored low on shared non-negotiable values, try to identify which specific values do not match. Then consider whether these non-negotiable values can be bridged with understanding. Remember, if you nag your spouse to change, you will only increase the conflict. Work to bridge the differences between non-negotiable values.

If for one of you the values that do not mesh are negotiable, define under what circumstances it would be helpful to modify them. Could they be modified when you are in a social gathering? Professional setting? With extended family? Determine whether modifying, as well as bridging, is a viable option for you as a couple.

If you scored five or below on any other dimension–empathy, assertiveness, unconditional love, or compromise–each can be strengthened through self-help books, classes, or counseling. To learn, grow, and change are part of a vital marriage. Any or all of these dimensions can be improved.

With these concepts and skills in mind, let's return to Betsy and Ben, Tricia and Tom. As we have already seen, Betsy and Ben share similar values, have the skills of empathy and assertiveness, love each other unconditionally, and are able to compromise to a win/win resolution. Their respective Relationship Evaluation forms would reflect the strength of their marriage.

Betsy's Relationship Evaluation Form

Please consider yourself and your partner as a couple on items 1 through 4. The number you select is a team score.

On the last two items, 5a and 5b, which are related to conditional and unconditional love, score yourself and your partner individually.

For every item, 1 is low and 10 is high.

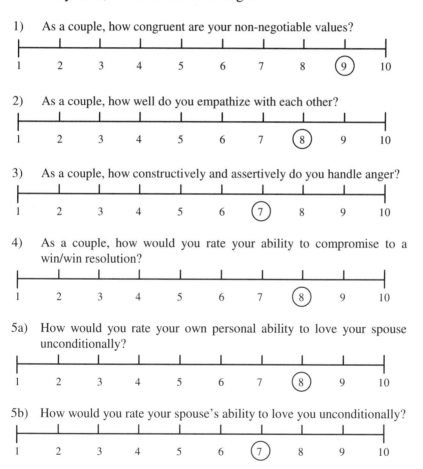

1)   As a couple, how congruent are your non-negotiable values?

1   2   3   4   5   6   7   8   ⑨   10

2)   As a couple, how well do you empathize with each other?

1   2   3   4   5   6   7   ⑧   9   10

3)   As a couple, how constructively and assertively do you handle anger?

1   2   3   4   5   6   ⑦   8   9   10

4)   As a couple, how would you rate your ability to compromise to a win/win resolution?

1   2   3   4   5   6   7   ⑧   9   10

5a)   How would you rate your own personal ability to love your spouse unconditionally?

1   2   3   4   5   6   7   ⑧   9   10

5b)   How would you rate your spouse's ability to love you unconditionally?

1   2   3   4   5   6   ⑦   8   9   10

Ben's Relationship Evaluation Form

Please consider yourself and your partner as a couple on items 1 through 4. The number you select is a team score.

On the last two items, 5a and 5b, which are related to conditional and unconditional love, score yourself and your partner individually.

For every item, 1 is low and 10 is high.

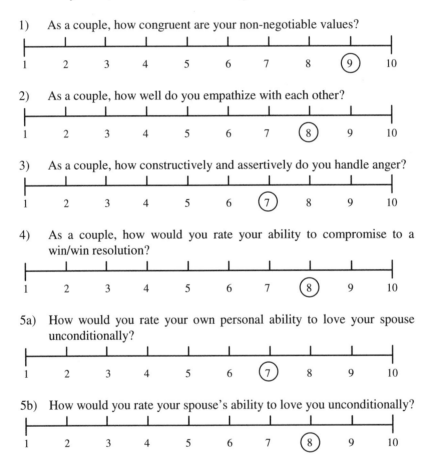

1)   As a couple, how congruent are your non-negotiable values?

   1   2   3   4   5   6   7   8   ⑨   10

2)   As a couple, how well do you empathize with each other?

   1   2   3   4   5   6   7   ⑧   9   10

3)   As a couple, how constructively and assertively do you handle anger?

   1   2   3   4   5   6   ⑦   8   9   10

4)   As a couple, how would you rate your ability to compromise to a win/win resolution?

   1   2   3   4   5   6   7   ⑧   9   10

5a)   How would you rate your own personal ability to love your spouse unconditionally?

   1   2   3   4   5   6   ⑦   8   9   10

5b)   How would you rate your spouse's ability to love you unconditionally?

   1   2   3   4   5   6   7   ⑧   9   10

While Betsy and Ben flourish, Tricia and Tom struggle. As we have discussed, they have significant stresses in all of the areas we have reviewed. Hence, their love for each other has been strained. The broken arrows on their forms reflect the slippage downward over the years.

Tricia's Relationship Evaluation Form

1) As a couple, how congruent are your non-negotiable values?

2) As a couple, how well do you empathize with each other?

3) As a couple, how constructively and assertively do you handle anger?

4) As a couple, how would you rate your ability to compromise to a win/win resolution?

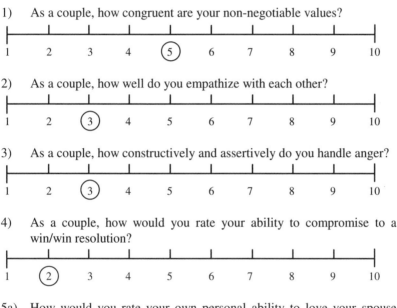

5a) How would you rate your own personal ability to love your spouse unconditionally?

Later ◀-------------------------------- Earlier

5b) How would you rate your spouse's ability to love you unconditionally?

Later ◀-- Earlier

Tom's Relationship Evaluation Form

1)   As a couple, how congruent are your non-negotiable values?

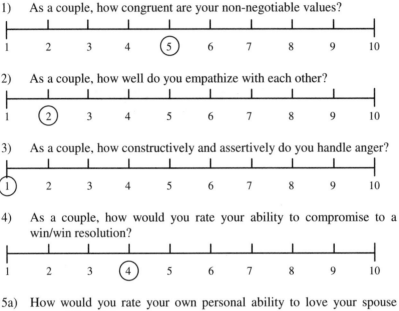

1   2   3   4   ⑤   6   7   8   9   10

2)   As a couple, how well do you empathize with each other?

1   ②   3   4   5   6   7   8   9   10

3)   As a couple, how constructively and assertively do you handle anger?

①   2   3   4   5   6   7   8   9   10

4)   As a couple, how would you rate your ability to compromise to a win/win resolution?

1   2   3   ④   5   6   7   8   9   10

5a) How would you rate your own personal ability to love your spouse unconditionally?

Later ◄--- Earlier

1   2   ③   4   5   6   7   8   ⑨   10

5b) How would you rate your spouse's ability to love you unconditionally?

Later ◄------------------------------- Earlier

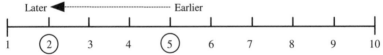

1   ②   3   4   ⑤   6   7   8   9   10

As is apparent, Tricia and Tom's marriage is in deep trouble. All of their scores are five or below.

As you live within your marriage and evaluate it on the Relationship Evaluation Form, you, like Tricia and Tom, may realize that your relationship is in jeopardy. If so, please consider counseling so that your scores can be upgraded and your marriage can become more intimate. It is never too late to learn and grow.

OPERATION

CHAPTER 7

VULNERABILITY VERSUS AFFAIRS

When a marriage is built on the five components of shared non-negotiable values, empathy, assertiveness, unconditional love, and compromise, emotional intimacy grows stronger over time. The couple creates a safe environment, a place where any feelings or issues can be discussed without fear of judgment or recrimination.

During Betsy and Ben's courtship, they began to develop this type of safe environment. For example, when they traveled to Madison to organize Ben's apartment, Ben learned it was permissible to share his self-doubt. Betsy listened with empathy and loved him unconditionally. She supported and encouraged him. She continued to believe in him. In turn, he provided the same type of atmosphere for her.

With the five components in place, the environment is safe and so too is vulnerability. Whatever is discussed is heard without judgment and remains confidential. Neither spouse turns any sensitive information against the other in a moment of anger. Their love for each other is consistent and unconditional.

Within this context, not only emotional but also sexual intimacy is comfortable. Neither Betsy nor Ben is tempted to have an affair. Neither is foolish enough to jeopardize their strong, life-giving marriage. Both are fully invested in the relationship.

In contrast, Tricia and Tom are in a very different situation. With the necessary components marginal or absent, whatever safety and vulnerability as well as emotional intimacy they had are now gone. They are roommates who simply have two children in common. They have a functional rather than an emotionally intimate relationship.

Vulnerability and self-disclosure are absent. Emotional intimacy is gone, as is sexual closeness. If sexual contact occurs, it happens by habit. It is no longer an expression of a loving relationship. Tom and Tricia live in an emotional and sexual vacuum. Hence, both are highly susceptible to an affair. Inadvertently the emptiness can be filled by a third person.

VULNERABILITY: DEFINITION

Vulnerability is the willingness to share your innermost self with someone else. It best occurs in a safe environment. When your scores are six or above as measured on the Relationship Evaluation Form, you have an environment conducive to sharing. The relationship is maintained and grows stronger and deeper over time. You both are able to reveal your most private and personal thoughts and feelings without fear of recrimination.

In such a marriage, you know you will be heard non-judgmentally and loved unconditionally. It is safe to share. Safety is a critical factor, because once your spouse knows your shortcomings and most private fears, anxieties, hopes, and dreams, your mate has the power to reject and hurt as well as accept and support you.

VULNERABILITY: CONTINUUM

Safety and vulnerability go hand in hand. As safety increases, so too does vulnerability. If a relationship proves trustworthy, self-disclosure can be increased. If it proves untrustworthy, it can be decreased.

Vulnerability can be conceptualized as a continuum, as the following diagram illustrates.

Vulnerability Continuum

Vulnerability

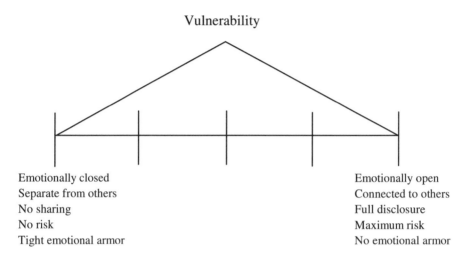

Emotionally closed
Separate from others
No sharing
No risk
Tight emotional armor

Emotionally open
Connected to others
Full disclosure
Maximum risk
No emotional armor

As suggested by this continuum, you can choose the degree to which you wish to share with any given person. You can be totally or somewhat private, totally or somewhat disclosing. For example,

> You can share only pleasantries as you might with an acquaintance: Isn't the weather hot? The Pittsburgh Pirates did a great job last night.

> You could share only general personal information as you might with a casual friend: I am married with two grown children.

> You could share general feelings like you might with a somewhat closer friend: My oldest daughter went off to college today and I'm feeling very mixed emotions. I guess it's the empty nest syndrome.

You might share more private and personal feelings as you would with a very close friend: It's the anniversary of my mother's death and I feel overwhelmed with grief. Life is lonely without her.

You might share the deepest, most private thoughts and feelings as you would with your intimate other: I feel very jealous about his promotion. I am so envious I can hardly bear it. Yet I feel ashamed of myself. I am really torn and upset.

The diagram that follows illustrates these various points on the continuum. Safety determines your degree of self-disclosure.

Points On The Vulnerability Continuum

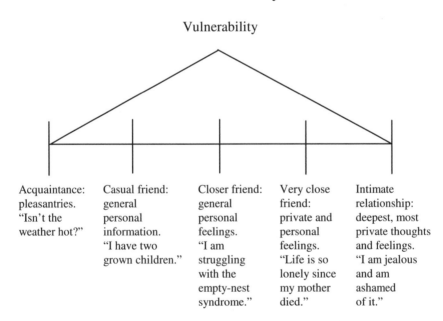

| Acquaintance: pleasantries. "Isn't the weather hot?" | Casual friend: general personal information. "I have two grown children." | Closer friend: general personal feelings. "I am struggling with the empty-nest syndrome." | Very close friend: private and personal feelings. "Life is so lonely since my mother died." | Intimate relationship: deepest, most private thoughts and feelings. "I am jealous and am ashamed of it." |

You have a choice as to the degree of self disclosure with which you operate in any given relationship. How do you decide when it is safe to move up the continuum and increase vulnerability?

If you are already in a significant relationship, think about how it developed. In all likelihood, as you dated, it became increasingly apparent that your partner practiced empathy, assertiveness, unconditional love, and compromise, and shared the same non-negotiable values. Consequently, you felt safer, took increased risk, and shared more and more. You moved up the continuum and became more emotionally open. You increasingly laid aside your protective armor.

Perhaps you can recall how your partner proved safe on each of the five dimensions. Did your mate listen to you with non-judgmental understanding and heartfelt concern? (Empathy) Share feelings constructively and in an assertive manner? (Assertiveness) Love you even when you made mistakes? (Unconditional love) Resolve issues in a mutually satisfactory way? (Compromise)

Did your spouse share your non-negotiable values? For example, did your partner operate in an honest fashion, keep promises, and maintain confidentiality–values which are critical to you? Did your mate share your commitment to a self-disciplined and goal-oriented life? Did your partner exercise compassion? As these values were practiced, you learned the core of your mate. (Shared non-negotiable values) You saw the road map your mate used to navigate through life.

Over time, you determined it was safe to be increasingly open. As your partner lived out the five components, you moved up the continuum.

It should be noted that some people are tempted to use the light switch method with vulnerability. They disclose everything or nothing. The switch is either on or off. Because this system disallows adequate evaluation, it is rather dangerous. The person with whom you have shared may lack several or all of the five dimensions. Openness may be unsafe.

Wisdom lies in using the rheostat method, whereby you responsibly assess the other person on the five components and increase or decrease your self-disclosure accordingly. The more accomplished the other is in terms of empathy, assertiveness, unconditional love, and compromise, and the closer the other person's non-negotiable values mesh with yours, the safer it is to progress up the continuum. Be thoughtful as you consider a move upward. Once you share your innermost thoughts and feelings with someone, that person has the power to harm as well as help you.

VULNERABILITY: YARDSTICK

In order to determine how open to be with any given person, the five dimensions become the critical criteria. Together they make up the yardstick by which you measure the degree of safety for the sake of self-disclosure.

For example, if along with empathy, assertiveness, unconditional love and compromise, your personal non-negotiable values include honesty, keeping promises, confidentiality, self-discipline, goal-directedness, and compassion, these make up your yardstick. The diagram that follows illustrates.

Yardstick For Vulnerability

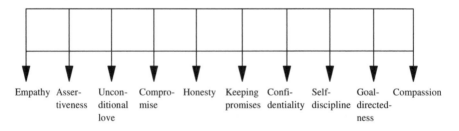

As discussed in Chapter 1, values differ from person to person. Therefore, yardsticks will vary as well. On the one that follows, empathy, assertiveness, unconditional love, and compromise are already noted. Please complete your personal yardstick. Refer back to your Value Clarification Chart on page 24 and add your particular non-negotiable values to your yardstick.

Personal Yardstick For Vulnerability

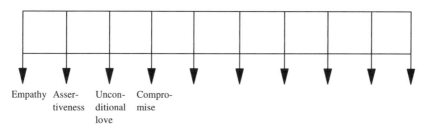

Empathy Asser- Uncon- Compro-
tiveness ditional mise
love

How well your partner measures up on your yardstick determines where you stop on the vulnerability continuum. With your yardstick, you can evaluate how safe it is to be open in any and all relationships.

The following vignette demonstrates how the vulnerability continuum and yardstick work. Dick and Sandy are college students who are in a serious relationship. On Dick's yardstick, there are several non-negotiable values, including confidentiality.

Dick tells Sandy that his friend Jerry's fiancee is pregnant. Therefore, the two of them plan to marry sooner than originally scheduled. Dick asks Sandy to keep this information confidential because they need time to discuss the situation with their parents and set the wedding date.

A few days later, Sandy's girlfriend asks Dick about Jerry's situation. Dick is stunned. When he checks with Sandy, she admits that she broke his confidence and told her girlfriend about the pregnancy and impending marriage.

Although Dick had been moving up the vulnerability continuum, at this point, he stops. As measured by his yardstick, Sandy has violated one of his cardinal non-negotiable values, the value of confidentiality. He has a decision to make. Will he give Sandy another chance? Or, will he share less, move down the continuum, and redefine the relationship as a more casual friendship?

You too can determine the appropriate degree of self-disclosure in your relationship. If your partner consistently meets the criteria on your yardstick, it is safe to move up the vulnerability continuum. As you do so, the relationship will become stronger and more emotionally intimate.

SEXUAL VULNERABILITY

When safety and vulnerability are present in a marriage, there is both emotional and sexual intimacy. The contrary is also true. If they are absent, there will be emotional and sexual distance. Thus, when a couple comes into marriage counseling with the complaint of no sex, the first thing that needs to be evaluated is the degree of safety, vulnerability, and emotional intimacy. This can be done via the Relationship Evaluation Form. If any of the five components is askew, safety is negatively impacted, self-disclosure decreases, emotional closeness declines, and so too does sexual intimacy.

As we discuss sexual intimacy, it is important to note that there can be a difference between spouses in their need for safety, vulnerability, and emotional closeness in the sexual dimension. Frequently, this difference divides along gender lines. Often, the female partner requires all three in order to enjoy comfortable and pleasurable love-making. If these decrease, so too does sexual intimacy.

This connection between safety, vulnerability, and emotional closeness on the one hand and sexual intimacy on the other may have something to do with a woman's sex organs being internal and a man's being external. When a woman has sexual intercourse, she is maximally vulnerable and gives the ultimate of herself. Figuratively speaking, she allows her partner to touch her soul. For her to give to this degree, the relationship must be extremely safe and close. The following diagram illustrates.

Female Sexual Expression

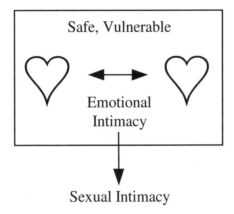

Sexual Intimacy

Although the male partner might prefer this same environment, he can appreciate sex not only when the relationship is harmonious but also during times of stress. In fact, being sexual may, for the male, facilitate the resolution of the issue causing the tension. The following diagram illustrates.

Male Sexual Expression

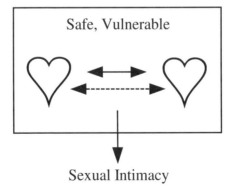

Sexual Intimacy

An example will illustrate this difference. Doug and Denise have a tiff at 5:00 p.m. It is not yet resolved by 8:00 p.m. when she walks through the living room in her negligee. She looks lovely. Doug proposes going to bed together. She indignantly indicates there is no way that will happen until the disagreement is resolved.

For her, there is a direct connection between the emotional state of the relationship and her desire to be sexual. She must feel safe and close in order to want to be sexual. Emotional intimacy is a prerequisite for sexual intimacy. Her husband, however, is able to separate the two. He can enjoy being sexual and resolve the tiff later. In fact, love-making actually might better enable him to settle the disagreement.

For her, first comes the harmonious relationship and then sex. Making love requires that the relationship be close, safe, and vulnerable. With emotional tension, the relationship feels disconnected. It is incongruent to be sexual. For him, however, sex can be appreciated with or without the issue resolved.

There is another sexual difference which generally divides along gender lines. Whereas women like to cuddle for the sake of closeness, men often see cuddling as foreplay. This disparity may lead to conflict. Whereas she simply wants to be affectionate, he anticipates intercourse.

Just as value differences need to be bridged or modified, so too with sexual differences. In the sexual dimension, both spouses need to bridge with understanding, and modify wherever possible. This is part of the challenge of marriage. In a safe, vulnerable, close relationship designed and built on the five components, these sexual differences can be constructively bridged and modified.

AFFAIRS

When the components discussed in this book are present, safety and vulnerability are facilitated. Emotional and sexual intimacy occur. When any one of the dimensions is askew, trustworthiness and vulnerability are hampered. Distance increases. Tricia and Tom's marriage is a good example.

Neither of them knew exactly what was wrong or how to fix it. They only knew that things were not going well and that they were not best friends. They had a functional rather than an intimate relationship. With the increase in emotional and sexual distance over time, the marriage became a very lonely place. Even though both believed in faithfulness and commitment, both were susceptible to an affair.

Often affairs happen slowly and subtly. For example, you and your friend innocently begin to talk. As you spend time together, the five components are in place. Your friend measures up on your yardstick. Safety and vulnerability increase. Eventually, not only emotional but also sexual intimacy occurs.

Although you may have a guilty conscience because your behavior lies outside of your non-negotiable values, you are caught between a troubled, lonely marriage and an emotionally and sexually vital relationship. The diagram that follows illustrates how distance occurs and an outside relationship happens.

How Affairs Occur

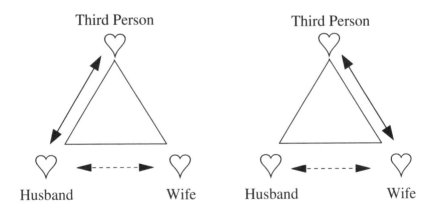

Because of the closeness and intensity with the third person, it may be a temptation to divorce your spouse and marry the other person. However, if either you or your mate wishes to make a present affair into a permanent relationship, you will want to consider what you leave behind: children, relationships with each other's extended family, and memories which include shared pain and accomplishments. Further, you need to evaluate the same issues discussed in the previous chapters. Over the long term, do the two of you truly have the ability to practice empathy, assertiveness, unconditional love, and compromise? Do you have shared non-negotiable values?

If, after this evaluation, you decide to stay in your marriage, you and your spouse will need to do several things. First, diagnose the trouble spots in your marriage via the Relationship Evaluation Form. Second, based on this evaluation, focus on the areas that must be improved or the values that must be bridged or modified. To do this on your own is a tall order. It might be wiser to enter therapy to ensure that the necessary changes can be accomplished successfully.

Let's return to Tricia and Tom. As measured by the Relationship Evaluation Form, their scores are five or below on every item. It is apparent that it is unsafe for either of them to share and be vulnerable with each other emotionally or sexually.

In addition to the fact that several significant non-negotiable values are mismatched, they do not share feelings in a heart-to-heart, empathetic way. They do not constructively handle anger and other emotions. They are not assertive. From the onset, Tricia loved Tom conditionally, and, as the marital stress and discord increased, Tom began to love Tricia in the same way.

Their most significant attempt to compromise was done in regard to geographic location, but over the years that decision felt to Tricia like a win/lose resolution. Her career goals were not met. Increasingly, she became angry with and uninterested in Tom and his career. Their only shared interest was their children.

The components necessary for safety and vulnerability were absent. Hence, the relationship lacked emotional and sexual intimacy. Feelings were not shared verbally or sexually. Tricia and Tom had become roommates who split expenses and child-rearing tasks. Both of them were susceptible to an affair, although neither realized it. When the trap sprang on Tom, the marriage came to a screeching halt. They decided to enter therapy in an attempt to evaluate and resolve the problems.

It is not uncommon that an affair is the crisis that propels couples into counseling. At this point, they must assess the trouble spots within the marriage via the Relationship Evaluation Form. They must look at their respective parts in the marital breakdown and be willing to learn new skills. Then, when the five components are in place, safety and vulnerability can be increased, and emotional and sexual intimacy can be nurtured.

Thereafter, the focus can shift to forgiveness. First, they will need to forgive themselves and each other for their shortcomings. Then they will need to forgive the partner who had the affair. All of this is no small feat. The next chapter will focus on the challenge of forgiveness.

REPAIR

CHAPTER 8

FORGIVENESS

Although an affair is very painful and destructive to a relationship, invariably it is a symptom and not the cause of the marital breakdown. More than likely, the source of the difficulty is one or more of the five components being askew. With this stress, safety and vulnerability have decreased and, likewise, emotional and sexual intimacy. Simultaneously, the danger of an affair has increased. Tricia and Tom's relationship demonstrates how this distance occurs and an affair happens.

In contrast, Ben and Betsy's relationship illustrates the opposite. With the five components in place, the marriage becomes stronger over time. Safety and vulnerability increase. Emotional and sexual intimacy occurs comfortably and consistently. That is not to say that neither of them will ever be attracted to someone else. However, since the relationship is vigorous and operates smoothly, they will be reluctant to trade the certainty of a vital marriage for the uncertainty of an affair. When a marriage is emotionally and sexually close and spouses are best friends, neither is likely to pursue an outside relationship. Commitment is willingly maintained.

BLAME VERSUS RESPONSIBILITY

Even though an affair is the result rather than the cause of a marital breakdown, it is very destructive and needs to be addressed and adequately resolved if the marriage is to continue. Because resolution can be difficult and complex, it is often best done in therapy. Initially, both partners need to forgive themselves and each other. They must exercise personal and interpersonal forgiveness. Thereafter, each must forgive the offending partner in order to move beyond the affair.

In order to complete the process of personal and interpersonal forgiveness and eventually forgiveness of Tom for the affair, Tricia and Tom need to understand where each one fell short on the five dimensions and what they need to change. The Relationship Evaluation Form is the beginning point. The results will help them see how they each experienced the marriage. The weak areas will be apparent. Whether they ultimately save or dissolve the relationship, counseling will help them understand why the marriage floundered. They both contributed. Although it is a temptation to blame each other or the third person, blame is dead-end. As long as they finger-point, forgiveness is disallowed.

Instead, it is essential that both partners understand their respective contribution to the breakdown of the relationship. Then they can assume their own responsibility and stop accusing their mate. The transition from blame to responsibility is essential if forgiveness is to occur. If either spouse continues to point the finger, personal and interpersonal forgiveness as well as forgiveness of the partner who had the affair is precluded.

If the offended spouse continues to blame, the affair will be revisited ad nauseam. It will be used as a vicious weapon. It will disallow rebuilding the marriage on the five components, developing safety and vulnerability, and revitalizing emotional and sexual intimacy. If the marriage ends and accusations continue after the divorce, the result will be ongoing bitterness and hostility. The spouse who continues to blame will have little time, energy, or emotional space to love someone else.

As Tricia and Tom become involved in therapy, they will understand their respective contribution to the marital breakdown. As the therapist works with them as a couple and dissects their patterns of communication, each will more clearly understand his or her part. Neither Tricia nor Tom practiced empathy, assertiveness, and compromise. Tricia did not share her feelings constructively and assertively. Her sarcasm and cutting comments eventually drove a wedge between the two of them. Further, from the outset, she loved Tom conditionally.

Tom contributed, too. Early on, he stopped being empathetic and assertive. He withdrew and distanced himself. His unconditional love waned. Further, neither of them clearly understood nor addressed the differences in their non-negotiable values.

They each participated in the marital breakdown and must realize and accept their parts. Although both were susceptible to an affair, Tom succumbed. The affair precipitated the crisis that brought them into counseling. Now the difficulties can be identified and resolved.

After they both assume their respective responsibilities, they are ready to address the issue of personal forgiveness, interpersonal forgiveness, and forgiveness of Tom and his affair. In order to avoid getting stuck on blame about the affair, personal responsibility and personal forgiveness must occur first. Tom and Tricia together created a relationship which functioned poorly. The affair is not excused but rather is dealt with in the larger context of the troubled marriage in which both partners fell short.

Forgiveness–whether personal, interpersonal, or forgiveness of the partner who had the affair–is a form of problem-solving. It involves the steps described in Chapter 2. Please review the diagram on page 52.

Step one involves knowledge of the facts. The Relationship Evaluation Form, along with therapy, enables Tricia and Tom to know where and how they individually and jointly fell short. As they proceed with therapy, they can identify and understand more specifically their respective shortcomings. Each contributed to the marital breakdown.

In step two, they can get in touch with the related feelings. Each needs to fully feel emotions of anger, disappointment, hurt, and sadness about their own shortcomings as well as those of their spouse. The relationship is struggling because of both of them individually and jointly, and now a destructive affair has occurred.

Often with forgiveness, it is a temptation to skip step two and jump to step three, which involves generating options and making the decision to forgive. However, if forgiveness is to be maintained over time, the emotions must be adequately experienced. When the feelings have been felt long enough and deeply enough, it is time to move into step three. The head and heart talk things over, develop options, make the decision to forgive, and then act on it.

Personal Forgiveness

Both Tricia and Tom need to go through the process of personal forgiveness. Tricia must appreciate that she was sarcastic and loved Tom conditionally. Her values were different than his, and these differences were neither successfully bridged nor modified. She needs to feel the sadness about the lost years of her marriage. She has been lonely, hurt, and angry over this period. Instead of its being entirely Tom's fault, she must understand that she too contributed. She needs to allow herself to feel these feelings long enough and deeply enough so that when she chooses to forgive herself, she can maintain that forgiveness. Only she can determine when she has felt enough. Feeling enough varies from person to person and issue to issue, but feeling enough is critical.

After she knows the facts about her contribution to the marital breakdown and feels the related emotions of anger, sadness, and regret, her head and heart can dialogue, generate options, and reach the decision to forgive herself. Her internal conversation might sound like this.

The facts are: I did not share my feelings constructively and assertively but rather was sarcastic. My
love for Tom was conditional, and our values did
not mesh. I have not been a good marriage partner. I
couldn't and didn't do my part of the relationship
well. I was neither a partner nor a friend.

The emotions are: My heart is filled with overwhelming sadness, loss, grief, and disappointment
about all of this. It has been an unsafe relationship
which lacked vulnerability as well as emotional and
sexual intimacy. I have been robbed and so has
Tom. The best thing about the relationship is our
two children.

Then options are developed: What shall I do? I
could refuse to change. I could forgive myself and
focus on learning from this pain. I could further
clarify my non-negotiable values and practice
empathy, assertiveness, unconditional love, and
compromise.

Ultimately, a decision is made and action is taken:
I'll forgive myself and focus on learning from this
pain. I'll clarify my non-negotiable values and seek
to practice empathy, assertiveness, unconditional
love, and compromise.

In summary, forgiveness involves the steps of problem-solving.
The facts must be known, the feelings felt, the options developed, a
decision made, and action taken. The diagram that follows illustrates
Tricia's process of personal forgiveness.

Tricia's Process of Personal Forgiveness

1) ◯ ——▶ Facts: I have lacked the ability to exercise
                                empathy, assertiveness, unconditional love,
                                and compromise. My non-negotiable values
                                are different than Tom's.

2) ♡ ——▶ Feelings: I feel sadness, grief, loneliness, and anger
                                about my deficiencies and what I and we
                                were unable to experience together as a
                                couple.

3) ◯   Develop Options: I could
                                - refuse to change.
                                - forgive myself.
                                - focus on learning from this pain.

   ♡   Make a Decision: Forgive myself.
                                Focus on learning from this pain.

            Take Action: Clarify my non-negotiable values.
                                Practice empathy, assertiveness,
                                unconditional love, and compromise.

If you struggle because a third person has entered your relationship, you can appreciate Tricia and Tom's pain from a personal perspective. You know firsthand that when there is an affair it is difficult to focus on your personal contribution to the marital breakdown. It is an incredible stretch to deal with your own shortcomings and forgive yourself when the desire to blame your spouse and the third person is extremely intense. It is an almost overwhelming temptation to succumb to finger-pointing.

If you yield, however, forgiveness will be precluded, intimacy will be disallowed, and bitterness will fill your heart and rob you of future happiness. As the first step toward healing, you need to know your own deficiencies, experience the related emotions, and reach the decision to forgive yourself.

With personal and interpersonal forgiveness, and especially with forgiveness of the person who had the affair, if you find you cannot maintain your decision and take the action you determined to do, you may not have felt the feelings deeply enough or long enough. If this is the case, repeat the process until your decision holds fast. You may need to walk through the steps several times.

It is helpful to note that when Jesus Christ discusses forgiveness in the Bible, He states we are called on to forgive seventy times seven times (Matthew 18:21, 22). Hence, if you need to repeat the process, it does not mean you have not genuinely decided to forgive. Rather, it suggests that you have not felt enough to maintain your decision.

Tricia's process of personal forgiveness needed to be redone several times before it remained steadfast. The following diagram illustrates the repetition of her process to the point of completion.

Tricia's Process of Personal Forgiveness–Feeling Enough

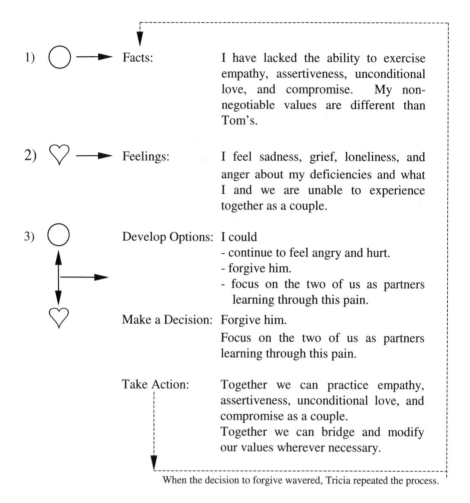

1) Facts: I have lacked the ability to exercise empathy, assertiveness, unconditional love, and compromise. My non-negotiable values are different than Tom's.

2) Feelings: I feel sadness, grief, loneliness, and anger about my deficiencies and what I and we are unable to experience together as a couple.

3) Develop Options: I could
- continue to feel angry and hurt.
- forgive him.
- focus on the two of us as partners learning through this pain.

Make a Decision: Forgive him.
Focus on the two of us as partners learning through this pain.

Take Action: Together we can practice empathy, assertiveness, unconditional love, and compromise as a couple.
Together we can bridge and modify our values wherever necessary.

When the decision to forgive wavered, Tricia repeated the process.

Although we have focused on Tricia's process of personal forgiveness, Tom needs to complete the same steps and forgive himself. He was not empathetic and assertive. He withdrew and distanced himself. He did not love Tricia unconditionally. As the therapist assists Tom to see his part in the destructive patterns, this enables him to identify more clearly his contribution to the marital breakdown.

INTERPERSONAL FORGIVENESS

As Tricia and Tom do joint therapy, they come to appreciate both their own and their mate's contribution to the dissolution of the relationship. Both fell short.

They need to forgive not only themselves for their respective contributions to the marital breakdown, but also each other. As they do marital counseling, they become aware of their mate's shortcomings as well as their own. In addition to personal forgiveness, Tricia and Tom need to exercise interpersonal forgiveness. The process is similar.

Tricia needs to know and feel the emotions about each of Tom's inadequacies. As with personal forgiveness, she needs to feel enough. Then she can generate options, make the decision to forgive him, and take the corresponding action. The diagram that follows clarifies Tricia's process of interpersonal forgiveness wherein she chooses to forgive Tom for his deficiencies. He needs to do the same in terms of forgiving her.

Tricia's Process of Interpersonal Forgiveness

1) ◯ ——▶ Facts: Tom has not exercised the skills of
                                empathy, assertiveness, unconditional love,
                                and compromise. His non-negotiable
                                values have been different than mine.

2) ♡ ——▶ Feelings: I feel angry and hurt that he has not been
                                my best friend and full partner in this
                                relationship. He has let me down.

3) ◯   Develop Options: I could
                                - continue to feel angry and hurt.
                                - forgive him.
                                - focus on the two of us as partners learning
                                  through this pain.

    ♡   Make a Decision: Forgive him.
                                Focus on the two of us as partners learning
                                through this pain.

            Take Action: Together we can practice empathy,
                                assertiveness, unconditional love, and
                                compromise as a couple.
                                Together we can bridge and modify our
                                values wherever necessary.

As Tricia forgives Tom's shortcomings, she recognizes that neither as individuals nor as a couple did they have the necessary skills to develop the safe and vulnerable relationship necessary for emotional and sexual intimacy. She realizes they were up against insurmountable odds from the beginning. They had deficiencies individually and as a team. Thus, the responsibility for the marital breakdown rests with both of them, not just with Tom because he had the affair. The marriage was in deep trouble long before the infidelity occurred.

Tom too must come to the awareness that individually and as a couple they share the responsibility for the marital breakdown. This appreciation and acknowledgment of their personal and interpersonal appreciation and acknowledgment of their personal and interpersonal responsibility are crucial. Only when both have reached this point are they ready to deal with forgiveness for the affair. When they understand their own and their partner's contributions, they will be less apt to accuse and blame each other. Both were deficient, and both contributed to the marital dissolution. The affair is directly related to their individual and joint shortcomings.

As the therapist diagnoses the difficulties via the Relationship Evaluation Form and helps both partners appreciate their own and their spouse's shortcomings, personal and interpersonal forgiveness happens. Although both kinds of forgiveness are essential, they frequently occur quietly and privately within the heart of each of the partners. As they each work diligently to identify and resolve their own inadequacies, and see their spouse doing the same, they can forgive themselves and each other silently. Their desire to learn and grow facilitates the process of forgiveness.

In contrast to the rather subtle nature of personal and interpersonal forgiveness, forgiveness of the affair is a clear and defined focal point in therapy. One or more sessions are aimed at accomplishing this goal. It is mandatory if the relationship is to be restructured and renewed. It is required if the marriage is to continue and endure over time.

FORGIVENESS OF AN AFFAIR

Now Tricia and Tom are ready to turn their focus to the forgiveness of Tom for his affair. Infidelity is a difficult challenge to overcome. However, it must be surmounted if the marriage is to survive.

In order for both of them to forgive Tom's unfaithfulness, empathy is critical. They must empathetically enter into the other's pain and listen in a non-defensive manner as their mate reveals the personal devastation related to the affair.

In order to give Tricia relief from her pain so that eventually she can also listen to Tom, it is advisable to begin the process of forgiveness of the affair with her. She must share her pain while

Tom listens. He needs to enter into her intense hurt compassionately, be attentive, and listen quietly. In order to avoid defensiveness, she must use the skill of assertiveness. Tricia must speak using "I" messages and the sentence stem "I feel _____ because _____."

Tricia: "I feel hurt because we committed our lives to each other and have two beautiful children. I feel angry and betrayed because the affair was with my best friend.

I can hardly comprehend that this has happened, especially between the two people I have loved and valued the most. I am devastated and overwhelmed. How can we go on? How can I dare to trust you again?"

As the tears roll down Tricia's cheeks, Tom reaches into his pocket and lovingly hands her his handkerchief. Tom continues to listen empathetically and feel Tricia's pain with her. She speaks again.

"Some days I am so angry I never want to see you again. Other days I am overcome with grief and sadness. I see no way out of this situation. How can I ever forgive you?"

The process of forgiveness for the affair has begun. Tricia will need to say much, much more. Only when she has said enough and Tom truly has heard and felt her pain enough is it Tom's turn. When this point is reached, the process is reversed.

Tricia must listen empathetically and without judgment, just as Tom has done. As Tom begins to talk using "I" messages, Tricia learns that an affair is not as fun-filled and fancy-free as she has imagined. It has been devastating for Tom to violate his marital commitment and non-negotiable values. A guilty conscience has been an extremely heavy burden to bear. Tricia needs to feel the pain of all of this. She must hear the trauma and struggle as well as the intense personal disappointment and self-recrimination that Tom experiences.

Tom: When you talk about betrayal, I know what you mean. I feel like such a traitor, a traitor to our relationship, you, me, our children, and your friendship with your best friend. The guilt and self-hatred are beyond belief. I hope and pray you can forgive me, but I wonder if I'll ever be able to forgive myself.

Tom covers his face with his hands and weeps. Tricia looks extremely sad, reaches out, and touches his arm.

Tears are often a significant part of forgiveness and healing. Tricia and Tom cry for themselves, for each other, and for their relationship. As they listen to one another, they hear with their hearts. The two of them are connected on the heart level, and they empathetically feel each other's pain.

Few, if any, factual questions need to be asked or answered. Sometimes spouses think that to know the facts, including what was done sexually, would be helpful. Actually, these details often make it more difficult to forgive and move forward. It is not beneficial to ruminate about the specifics, but it is helpful to feel the pain and devastation related to the affair.

For some couples, there needs to be only one session like this; for others there must be several. An affair is a monumental issue, and the needs and feelings of each partner must be honored.

For any couple, including Tricia and Tom, these sessions happen only after adequate counseling wherein both mates are aware of their own and each other's parts in the marital breakdown and have experienced personal and interpersonal forgiveness. Only when they know that they individually and together bear the responsibility for the marriage difficulties can they grapple with the affair in a fruitful manner.

After partners understand the contributions they made individually and together, they can deal with the affair in the context of the larger picture. The marriage was in trouble because of both of them. The emotional and sexual distance between them was filled by a third person. The affair was the catalyst which brought the problems to light.

When Tricia and Tom each determine they have felt and shared enough, they can make the decision to forgive. The following diagram summarizes the process.

Tricia and Tom's Forgiveness of Tom's Affair

Tricia   **Tom**

Steps   Steps

1) ◯ ➤ Facts: 1) ◯ ➤ Facts:

Tom had an affair with   I had an affair with
my best friend.   Tricia's best friend.

2) ♡ ➤ Feelings: 2) ♡ ➤ Feelings:

For myself, I feel betrayal,   For myself, I feel
anger, and grief; the trust   devastated that I
is gone.   disappointed Tricia and
                                                 myself in such a significant
For Tom, I empathetically   way.
feel his devastation about
disappointing himself and   For her, I empathetically
me in such a significant way.   feel her betrayal, anger, and
                                                 grief; the trust is gone.

3) ◯ ⇅ ♡
 • Develop options:
  - blame.
  - forgive.
  - try to move forward.
  - divorce.
 • Make a decision:
  - forgive.
  - try to move forward.
 • Take action:
  - together practice empathy, assertiveness,
    unconditional love, and compromise.
  - together work to bridge our
    non-negotiable values.
  - re-discuss the affair constructively as
    often as either of us requires.

Often the timing on the decision to forgive varies from person to person. Tricia and Tom may not be perfectly synchronized. One may be ready sooner than the other.

If they make the decision to forgive but for one or both forgiveness does not remain constant, they may need to visit the issue again. Both partners need to feel the feelings deeply enough and long enough. They must feel to the extent that will allow the decision to forgive to remain steadfast.

It should be noted that even when the decision to forgive has held firm for some time, Tricia and Tom may need to feel additional pain and sadness from time to time, or they may need to re-discuss the affair and reaffirm the decision to forgive. To revisit does not mean that forgiveness has not occurred. It indicates that some additional feelings have bubbled to the surface and need to be felt and processed.

Frequently the offended spouse is the one who needs to return to the issue of the affair. For the partner who has committed the offense, this discussion is painful. However, love is long-suffering, and the process of forgiveness must be honored. Love means your spouse's needs are equally important to you as your own. To revisit the pain of the affair is difficult for both spouses, but it must be done. With time, there will be longer and longer periods between discussions, and the emotions themselves will be less and less intense.

The memory of the affair will not disappear. However, to live in a safer, more vulnerable, emotionally and sexually intimate relationship will help the pain fade. If Tricia and Tom decide to stay married, their insights about themselves and each other, their work on forgiveness, and their new patterns of interacting designed and built on the five components will serve them well. The marriage has been restructured. Time and practice will reinforce the positive changes. Success builds on success.

It should be acknowledged that to forgive yourself and your spouse for slippage on one or more of the five components is one thing. Forgiveness of an affair is quite another. This is a monumental challenge. This forgiveness becomes a mandatory and pivotal issue. When there is an affair, no matter how successful the personal and interpersonal forgiveness related to the five components, forgiveness of the affair is required for healing and continuation of the marriage. Without such forgiveness, it is difficult, if not impossible, to process the pain, let the memory fade, allow the new skills and behaviors to consolidate, and develop trust again.

It should be noted that trust is quickly lost and slowly regained. Tom's unfaithfulness destroyed it. It will take considerable time to rebuild it. Whether Tricia will ever trust him to the same degree is unknown. However, even though her trust of Tom might be more limited, it may be enough for the marriage to continue. Like scar tissue after surgery, although the skin looks and feels different, it is adequately strong. It may be possible for Tom and Tricia to move forward in the awareness that they are committed to their redesigned relationship.

An affair often motivates couples to enter counseling. They realize their marriage is in dire straits. They recognize they need to get help and make positive changes in the relationship or end it. With therapy, the trouble spots can be diagnosed, and both partners can assume their respective responsibility for the marital breakdown. They can forgive themselves, each other, and the partner who was involved in the affair. The necessary skills can be learned and practiced. The marriage can be saved and restructured.

Whether the marriage ultimately continues or ends, forgiveness frees each partner to move forward without blame, hostility, or bitterness. If Tricia and Tom decide to end the marriage, they can leave with less anger and a fuller appreciation of how each of them contributed to the marital breakdown. The more understanding and less blame that they feel, the greater the possibility that they can move into the future with a sense of clarity about the past and hope for the future.

In this chapter, the focus has been on forgiveness in a troubled marriage, particularly when an affair has occurred. However, it is important to recognize that in a strong, vital relationship, forgiveness is a regular, often unnoticed occurrence. In a marriage built on the five dimensions, forgiveness happens frequently and without conscious awareness. Each partner forgives without much effort or thought.

In Ben and Betsy's relationship, if Ben forgets to bring home a gallon of milk, he apologizes. Betsy thinks little of it and serves another beverage. If Betsy doesn't get the laundry done on schedule, she apologizes. Ben shrugs his shoulders and wears the same lab coat one more day. In a marriage that operates on the five components, the partners live a life of daily forgiveness.

CHAPTER 9

OPTIONS SHORT OF DIVORCE

Although counseling may prove helpful, sometimes, even with diligent effort on the part of both partners, the marriage remains marginal. If this is the case, the spouses are not compelled to file for divorce. There are other options.

We don't know yet what will happen with Tricia and Tom, but it is possible that even after they forgive, improve the five components, create an environment wherein it is safer to be vulnerable, and practice more emotional and sexual intimacy, it may be too late to have a solid marriage. If this is the case, rather than leave the relationship, they have at least three options short of divorce. They can supplement, do a working separation, or file for separate maintenance.

SUPPLEMENTING

Rather than end the marriage, they can supplement it with other emotionally fulfilling relationships and activities such as work, school, hobbies, and their children. Potentially, these involvements will give enough positive reinforcement and fulfillment that they will be able to remain in their less than ideal marriage.

If you are in a similar situation and desire to remain in your somewhat inadequate relationship, supplementing might be a desirable option. You may wish to keep an intact family for the sake of your children or because you have strong religious or financial reasons which compel you to stay. Supplementing with activities and involvements that give you emotional fulfillment allows you to stay in a marginal marriage for a time and perhaps indefinitely.

If you decide to continue in your marriage and supplement it, begin by clarifying the strengths and weaknesses of your relationship. Focus on what is present rather than what is absent. Appreciate your history together, your children, and your extended families. Stop expecting close emotional and sexual intimacy.

After this evaluation and adjustment, shift your focus to other people and activities. Look for emotional fulfillment elsewhere. You can get your needs met in various ways other than through your marriage. Volunteer at your children's school or a convalescent home, work in a job or career you enjoy, take classes, enter a degree program, or join a hiking club. The diagram that follows illustrates how supplementing works.

Supplementing

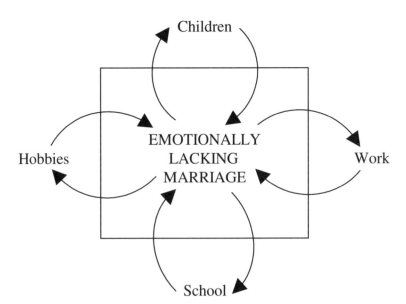

Supplementing in order to meet your emotional needs is clearly preferable to an affair. This method supports your marriage and family, whereas an affair undermines it. However, be aware that even though you opt for supplementing, you run the risk of having an extramarital relationship. As you are more emotionally involved outside of your home, you are bound to meet supportive people of the opposite sex. Close friendships will develop.

Supplementing is a coping mechanism. It does not remove your desire for an intimate relationship. Although you have altered the expectation that your spouse will meet your emotional needs, your heart still longs to be connected intimately with the heart of another. As you meet others who share your interests, friendships will grow. As the emotional connectedness increases, so too the risk of an affair.

Therefore, if you choose to remain in a less than ideal marriage and to support it by supplementing with constructive outside involvements, be aware that you are susceptible to an affair. Be forewarned so you can avoid potentially detrimental situations.

WORKING SEPARATION

If Tom and Tricia have worked diligently in therapy and have focused on assessment, forgiveness, and resolution and yet the relationship is going poorly, they have another option short of divorce. They can design and execute a working separation.

A working separation is different than the usual type of separation inasmuch as it is not done impulsively or out of anger. Instead, it is designed and executed thoughtfully. Together, both partners develop a plan for the purpose of trying one more time to breathe life into their marriage. Specific goals are set and a time line is established. Rather than a separation that happens out of frustration or resignation, it is arranged in a responsible manner and leaves the door wide open to reconciliation and recommitment. Often the plan is developed within the context of therapy.

If one of you is involved in an extramarital relationship, the therapist will ask you to table it until the working separation and related counseling have been completed. The following list represents the types of issues that are planned as part of a working separation:

- goals for the separation
- duration
- individual counseling plan, including specific goals
- joint counseling plan, including specific goals
- dating each other
- housing arrangements
- parenting schedule
- financial arrangements
- date for reassessment, both to determine if the goals for the separation have been attained and to decide what the next step will be.

The example which follows illustrates the format used and questions to be answered so a couple can establish the goal(s) and plan for a working separation.

Working Separation

Goal: to determine whether this marriage can be restructured and saved.*

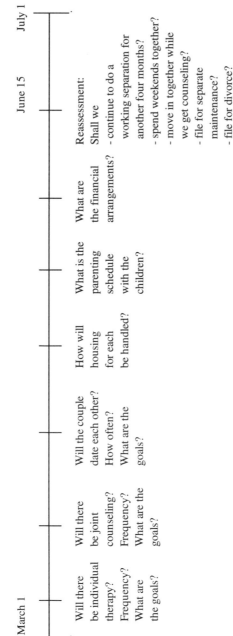

| March 1 | | June 15 | July 1 |

Will there be individual therapy? Frequency? What are the goals?

Will there be joint counseling? Frequency? What are the goals?

Will the couple date each other? How often? What are the goals?

How will housing for each be handled?

What is the parenting schedule with the children?

What are the financial arrangements?

Reassessment: Shall we
- continue to do a working separation for another four months?
- spend weekends together?
- move in together while we get counseling?
- file for separate maintenance?
- file for divorce?

*Any extramarital relationship is tabled until the working separation has been completed.

Perhaps some couples can establish the details of a working separation on their own. However, more often it is advisable to have a marriage counselor facilitate the discussion and planning as well as do the related therapy. To design and execute such a separation takes determination and a strong willingness to evaluate one last time whether the marriage can be saved. A competent therapist is a strong ally in this process.

While in counseling, Tricia and Tom decided to do a working separation. They developed the following plan.

Tricia and Tom's Working Separation

Goal: To make a decision regarding the marriage*

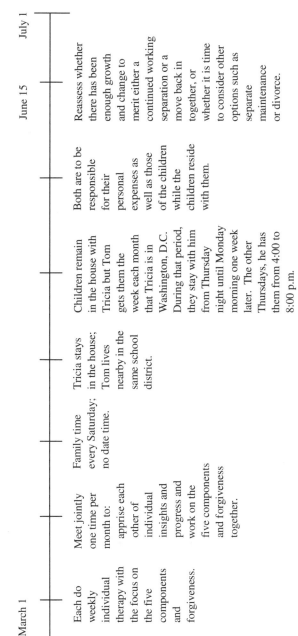

March 1			June 15	July 1

Each do weekly individual therapy with the focus on the five components and forgiveness.

Meet jointly one time per month to: apprise each other of individual insights and progress and work on the five components and forgiveness together.

Family time every Saturday; no date time.

Tricia stays in the house; Tom lives nearby in the same school district.

Children remain in the house with Tricia but Tom gets them the week each month that Tricia is in Washington, D.C. During that period, they stay with him from Thursday night until Monday morning one week later. The other Thursdays, he has them from 4:00 to 8:00 p.m.

Both are to be responsible for their personal expenses as well as those of the children while the children reside with them.

Reassess whether there has been enough growth and change to merit either a continued working separation or a move back in together, or whether it is time to consider other options such as separate maintenance or divorce.

*Tom had already terminated his relationship with the third person.

If the working separation is successful, Tom and Tricia may decide to remain married and to recommit to the relationship. If they discover that to be apart is a relief and it is too late for the marriage, separate maintenance is another option short of divorce. When they reassess on June 15, they may decide to consider this option.

SEPARATE MAINTENANCE

Separate maintenance would allow Tricia and Tom to stay married but be legally separated. If they wish to remain married for personal, professional, family, financial, or religious reasons, they can file for separate maintenance and live apart indefinitely.

Separate maintenance involves a judicial proceeding in which a court order is entered and legal separation occurs. It establishes such issues as custody of the children, child support payments, and division of assets. In most states, either spouse is free to opt for a divorce at a later time. The divorce action then supersedes the separate maintenance order.

As you and your spouse assess your particular situation, you may wish to consider this option. If you mutually decide you want to remain separated indefinitely and do not want a divorce, in all likelihood a request for separate maintenance can be filed. Check with the court in your particular state.

Thus, there are at least three options short of divorce which are available to you and your spouse. The first is supplementing, which facilitates your finding positive fulfillment in activities outside of the marriage. These involvements serve to supplement, at least for a time, a less than ideal relationship. The second is a working separation, which enables you and your spouse to set constructive guidelines for a time-limited physical separation so you can work on and reassess one more time whether the marriage can be saved. The third is separate maintenance, which allows you to stay married but live apart with a legal arrangement which covers custody, child support, and division of assets. Even when a marriage is marginal, there are options short of divorce.

BREAKDOWN

CHAPTER 10

DIVORCE: TRADITIONAL PROCESS VERSUS DIVORCE MEDIATION

TRADITIONAL DIVORCE PROCESS

If, after the working separation has been completed, Tricia and Tom determine that the marriage is not salvageable and they wish to pursue divorce, they can do so either through the traditional legal process or through divorce mediation. If they choose the traditional method, each retains a lawyer. Their respective attorneys assist them to work out the required agreements about such issues as custody, child support, spousal support if appropriate, and division of assets. They as mates are not to discuss these matters directly with one another but rather are to communicate only through their lawyers. The same guidelines would apply to you and your partner if you decide to divorce and use the traditional legal method.

When the lawyers secure an agreement between the two of you, the Judgment of Divorce is prepared and on the appointed day the judge finalizes it. If you do not reach agreement, your case will go to court and a judge will determine the outcome. In Michigan, the divorce process takes a minimum of six months if there are minor children, and two months if there are no children or if they are over the age of eighteen. Please check the rules and regulations in your particular state. The diagram that follows depicts how the traditional legal process works.

Traditional Legal Process

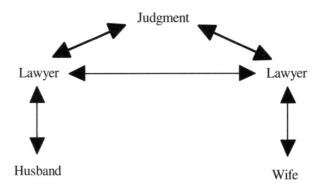

There are several reasons why this method may be a good choice for you. If your spouse is emotionally, physically, or sexually abusive or if your spouse is not trustworthy and honest, you may need all of the pressure and mechanisms that the legal system can bring to bear in order to disallow abuse and expose all of the facts, particularly the financial facts. Or, if you have not had any counseling and feel angry, bitter, and overwhelmed, you may want a forum in which you can fight and have a strong attorney advocate at your side. You may want your lawyer to be your gladiator with you and for you. Under any of these circumstances, the traditional legal process may be preferable.

However, if there is no need to ensure safety and truthfulness or if there is no desire to fight, the process may work against you. It may create unnecessary, intense, and expensive antagonism and misunderstanding.

Since in the traditional process any direct discussion between you as spouses is discouraged, you lose contact with each other and you lose control of the divorce process. If you participated in marriage counseling, you were encouraged to talk through difficult issues in a constructive manner. With the traditional legal method of divorce, that very type of communication is discouraged. Differences are not discussed and resolved between the two of you but rather are handled through your respective attorneys. Communication is complicated. Conflicts escalate.

You both speak only with your attorneys, and they in turn talk only to each other. The foregoing diagram illustrates the permissible lines of communication. This indirect contact, in which you and your spouse talk with each other exclusively through your respective lawyers, can result in misunderstanding, anger, additional financial cost, and an agreement with which you are not totally satisfied.

With the traditional legal process, your attorneys work out the agreement for the two of you, and the judge finalizes it. Since the communication process between you and your spouse is cumbersome and circuitous, the agreement is often less than ideal. Although your lawyers may be satisfied, you and your spouse may not be, and yet you will have to live with it. In an effort to modify the agreement, you and your spouse will need to return to court. In Michigan, you can change custody, visitation, and child support payments, but not the division of property. Litigation can go on until your youngest child turns eighteen.

As your marriage dissolves, you may feel as if your life is falling apart. Hence, it may be tempting to use the legal process of divorce and let the lawyers take over. However, once you give the communication process to your attorney, you relinquish considerable control over the eventual agreement that is reached.

DIVORCE MEDIATION PROCESS

In contrast, if Tricia and Tom choose divorce mediation, they select a process built on the component of compromise. With this method, Tricia and Tom talk to one another and resolve issues directly. They are empowered and in control. This will reduce conflict and increase cooperation in all areas, including co-parenting, throughout and after the divorce. The same is true for you if you and your spouse opt for this method.

If you use divorce mediation, the two of you will meet with either one divorce mediator, who is typically an attorney, psychologist, or social worker, or a team of two mediators, one an attorney and the other a helping professional. Since divorce is both a legal and emotional process, the team approach expedites both aspects.

The attorney knows the law and serves as an educator, legal consultant, and resource person. The lawyer is neutral and therefore does not represent either spouse. The psychologist or social worker helps you talk through your painful feelings so that agreements can be reached. With adequate information and emotional resolution, you can make mutually beneficial decisions. The diagram that follows illustrates.

Divorce Mediation Process

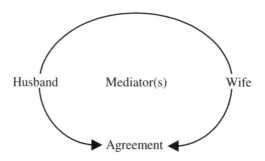

Husband   Mediator(s)   Wife

Agreement

The attorney mediator will write up the two resulting documents: a Memorandum of Agreement, which describes your arrangement in plain English, and a Judgment of Divorce, which formulates these same agreements in legal language and format.

Divorce mediation utilizes the compromise process described in Chapter 5. It is built on the same definition of love. Love is when your spouse's wants and needs, and now your children's as well, are equally important to you as your own. In divorce mediation, both spouses are committed to a win/win resolution for themselves and their children. They wish to end the marriage as amicably as possible and continue to co-parent in a complementary fashion.

Most couples who select mediation do so because they want a fair and equitable resolution of the financial and parenting issues. As a broad overview, the law basically requires a 50/50 split of the assets, a parenting arrangement in the best interest of the children, and child support in an amount that allows the children to continue enjoying a similar standard of living post-divorce.

Based on such factors as the number of years the mates have been married, whether one of them has been a full-time homemaker for an extended period of time, whether either has a significant and life-impacting health problem which negatively affects earning capacity, etc., alimony or spousal support may be deemed appropriate. The purpose of spousal support is to equalize the income for both partners.

In an effort to resolve all of these issues in mediation, the spouses will consider the wants and needs of each member of the family, develop a variety of options, and reach a win/win resolution for everyone involved. In divorce mediation, this is possible.

During the process, you and your spouse will decide if you wish to see an expert such as a CPA or real estate attorney. It is important that you have all of the necessary information available so you can make well-informed decisions. You will decide whether you should see the consultant together or if only one of you will go and then share the information at the next session. This is discussed and planned so there are no surprises. Surprises destroy trust, and trust is integral to divorce mediation. If one partner unexpectedly brings information from a consultant or outside attorney, it can be very destructive to the process. Both partners must be party to all discussions and decisions.

Although different mediators operate differently, there are several general aspects which are likely to occur. After an explanation of the mediation process, which includes a comparison with the traditional adversarial method, you will be asked to sign an agreement which contracts the services of the mediators. Since mediation is a voluntary process, you can always opt out. However, mediators generally request that if you wish to discontinue, you do so during a session so that the matter that seems insurmountable can be discussed. Perhaps with their assistance, you will be able to resolve the troublesome issue and continue and complete the divorce mediation process.

If you use the process, there are several other specifics which will occur. The mediators will ask you to fill out an asset and liability form. Often couples decide to do this together. Also, the mediators may suggest that each of you complete a budget form which will help you estimate what your new life as a single person and a single parent is going to cost.

In addition, they will encourage you and your spouse to think broadly and together formulate the ideal outcome of your divorce in terms of your assets, your relationship post-divorce, and your children. They will assist you in this process. The ideals you establish mutually are very important because they become the goals which you and the mediators wish to attain.

Examples of ideals related to assets might be as follows: We want to do the financial division so that the primary parent can keep the house until the youngest child turns eighteen. We want to divide the pension so that the spouse without a retirement plan has a nest egg for the future.

In terms of the relationship, your goals might include the following: We wish to be friends but respect each other's privacy as we develop separate lives. We want to continue attending the same church but will go to different services. We wish to maintain contact with each other's extended family but will be with them when our ex-spouse is not present.

In respect to the children, you might have the following ideals: We want our children to feel loved and parented by both of us even though we no longer

> live under the same roof. When the children are with one parent, we wish them to have easy telephone access to the other. We want to continue to make joint decisions about major issues related to the children.

As noted above, these ideals become the goals toward which you and the mediators strive. In all likelihood, you will be able to attain most if not all of them. Now, let's move forward and explore how the skill of compromise works within the framework of divorce mediation.

Imagine that the two of you are discussing assets and you wish to consider the issue of the house. You start with step one, wherein both of you list your wants and needs.

You state that you hope the house can remain a constant for the children during this time of transition. You share that you'd like them to have consistency in terms of the neighborhood, friendships, and school system. Your spouse indicates a desire for both of you to have an affordable house large enough to comfortably accommodate the children and in close proximity to one another so that the children can easily move between homes.

Then you move to step two and develop options. You consider refinancing the house, checking on real estate costs in the neighborhood with an eye toward buying a second home, or selling the house in order to purchase two smaller homes. The process to this point can be diagrammed as follows:

Sample Divorce Mediation Process

I. Wants/Needs:

In respect to the house, I'd like

You

1. it to remain a consistent part of the children's lives during this time of transition.
2. the children to stay in the neighborhood with their friends.
3. the children to remain in the same school district.

Your
Spouse

4. both of our homes to be large enough to accommodate the children.
5. both to be in reasonable proximity one to the other.
6. both to be affordable.

II. Options:

1. Check on the merits of refinancing the present house. Can any money be saved if we do so?
2. Check on housing costs in the area. Can a second house be purchased nearby at a reasonable cost?
3. Would it be financially wiser to sell the house and purchase two smaller homes elsewhere in the same school district?

Imagine that, as the idea of selling the house is mentioned, you are emotionally overwhelmed with a mixture of sadness, hurt, and anger. The tears begin to flow.

At this point, the communication switches from head-to-head to heart-to-heart. The psychologist/social worker would encourage you to identify your feelings and share them with your spouse. You'll be encouraged to talk assertively while your mate listens empathetically.

You: "I feel sad as I imagine such a dramatic change. I feel hurt and angry because I designed and decorated that house with you and our family in mind. You know better than anyone else the love and the attention to detail that went into that home. I feel devastated at the thought of selling it."

As the tears slip down your cheeks, your spouse listens, and then repeats back to you what you said. It is important that your partner hear your words and understand your feelings before responding.

Your Spouse: "I hear you saying you feel hurt and angry, because you lovingly designed and decorated the house. You feel devastated as we consider selling it."

And then it's your partner's turn to respond.

"I feel sad, too, sad because that dream along with the others related to our future has died. It is painful to dissolve our marriage. It overwhelms me to realize we will not live together in our house as a family until the children are grown."

Your spouse's eyes cloud with tears. There is a moment of silence.

If no more needs to be said and your feelings have been processed to the point where you both are able to move back into the head-to-head discussion related to the house, the mediation process continues.

It should be noted that the goal for marital therapy is different than for divorce mediation. In marriage counseling, the objective is to assess and upgrade the five dimensions so that vulnerability and intimacy can be maximized. Connection on the heart-to-heart level is more important than on the head-to-head level.

In divorce mediation, the head and heart levels are equally important. The goal is to reach a mutually acceptable agreement about your assets, future relationship, and children. Both levels of communication are facilitated at appropriate times so that agreements can be made and your divorce can be completed both legally and emotionally.

When the session ends, the options generated become the homework to be completed before the next session. You will explore refinancing, buying a second home in the neighborhood, and selling the house and buying two smaller homes elsewhere but in the same school district. You may decide to do this homework together, divide it and talk between sessions, or report back to each other at the next meeting.

Ultimately, the two of you will determine how to handle the house in a mutually satisfactory win/win manner. Your decision will be incorporated into the division of assets and written into both your Memorandum of Agreement and Judgment of Divorce.

The law requires that you make arrangements about division of assets, custody, child support payments, and possibly spousal support if the marriage is of a certain duration and other criteria are met. Concerning alimony, in Michigan, although the Washtenaw County Guidelines set forth the factors considered relevant in that county, there are no approved state-wide guidelines. You may wish to check in your state for the criteria used to determine if temporary or permanent spousal support is appropriate in your situation. Temporary alimony is short-term and designed for rehabilitation or re-entry into the job market. Permanent alimony is long-term.

In divorce mediation, couples often agree to things beyond these issues. For example, spouses may want to establish a method to finance a college fund for each of their children. Although in most states the law does not require this, it may be important to do so.

With regard to children, in divorce mediation, parenting is discussed within the context of co-parenting rather than custody and visitation. The words "custody" and "visitation" are emotionally laden and often incite negative feelings. The central issue is time spent with the children, and they need time with both parents.

The goal of divorce mediation is to determine the best and most workable plan for everyone involved, the children and both parents. A win/win co-parenting arrangement can be worked out when the needs of the children as well as the work schedules and unique contributions of both parents are considered. In the Memorandum of Agreement, the parenting arrangement will be described as you both establish it. However, in the Judgment of Divorce, which is the legal formulation of the arrangement, the words "custody" and "visitation" will reappear, since they are required. In the discussion which follows, the legal terms will be used to provide clarity.

Parenting involves two aspects, namely, physical custody and legal custody. Physical custody designates with whom the children will reside. It can be sole, joint, or split. Legal custody deals with who makes the major decisions regarding the children. Examples would include whether one of your children will be permitted to change schools, have elective surgery, or marry under age. Legal custody can be sole or joint, although joint is more common.

With a sole physical parenting arrangement or sole custody, the children have their home base with one parent and spend time on either a fixed or flexible schedule with the other. One parent has physical custody and the other visitation rights.

With fixed visitation, a specific schedule is established. For example, the parent with whom the children do not live might see them every other weekend, one evening each week, on alternating holidays, for half of both the Christmas and spring breaks, and during several weeks over the summer. In contrast, with flexible visitation, the parents together work out a mutually acceptable visitation schedule which may vary from week to week and year to year, depending on the needs and circumstances of the children as well as both parents. You and your partner may decide that, based on both the needs of the children and your respective lifestyles, sole physical custody is a wise parenting arrangement.

It should be noted that, with this arrangement, legal custody may be either sole or joint. If it is sole, the parent with whom the children reside is the one to make all of the major decisions. If it is joint, they make these decisions together.

With a joint physical parenting arrangement, the children live for alternating periods of time with each parent. For example, one parent may have the major parenting responsibility throughout the school year, and the other during the summer. When one parent is the primary caregiver, the other sees the children as desired or on a defined schedule. In the summer, the pattern is reversed. Another option might be to switch every four or six months. Or, each parent may be the major caregiver for different segments of the children's lives, based on the developmental stages of the children.

With a joint physical parenting arrangement, the parents have not only joint physical custody but also joint legal custody. Together they make the major decisions regarding their children.

The last type of parenting arrangement is known as split physical custody. Under such an arrangement, one or more children live primarily with one parent, and one or more live primarily with the other. For instance, the older children might live with their father and the younger with their mother, or vice versa. The parent with whom the children do not live on a regular basis would have visitation rights, which could be either fixed or flexible. In addition, the parties could have sole legal custody of the specific children they are parenting or joint legal custody for all of their offspring.

Based on the parenting plan you establish, child support is set. The type of custody and your respective incomes determine the dollar amount. In Michigan, tables are set forth in the *Child Support Manual*.

If your state has the same laws as Michigan, both your parenting arrangement and child support payments can be modified post-divorce if your life situation and income change. The process of changing custody may be straightforward if you as parents agree. You can use mediation to rework the parenting plan, and then either of your attorneys can file the necessary papers with the court.

However, if you as parents disagree, the matter becomes more complicated. You will need to go to court, and the judge will decide.

In contrast, once the assets are divided and finalized in the Judgment of Divorce, that division is permanent, unless there has not been full financial disclosure. Please review the rules and regulations in your specific state.

When all of the necessary decisions have been made and the process of divorce mediation is completed, the attorney mediator drafts the Memorandum of Agreement and the Judgment of Divorce. As noted earlier in this chapter, the Memorandum of Agreement states in common language the understandings you have reached. The Judgment of Divorce is the same set of agreements but written in legal language and in the required format.

Since mediators serve as neutral persons, an attorney mediator cannot be the lawyer who represents either of you. This is where other attorneys complement the process in very specific ways.

Sometime during the mediation process, an outside lawyer will need to file the initial complaint, which is the form that notifies the court of your intention to divorce. One of you will need to hire the attorney to initiate this process. At this point, that spouse becomes the Plaintiff. Although this may sound rather frightening or onerous, it simply means one of you has started the clock ticking. As previously discussed, each state requires a defined time period between filing and finalization of the divorce.

The date of filing can be discussed during mediation. There may be an advantage to waiting until you have made your agreements. In Michigan, when you file, the court requires temporary orders which set forth the plan for parenting your children. In all likelihood, you won't want to be pushed by the legal process to make premature decisions. Thus, it might be advisable to resolve these issues before starting the time clock.

At the conclusion of the mediation process and after the expiration of the required waiting period, the attorney who filed the complaint, along with the mate designated as the Plaintiff, will go to court to finalize the divorce. The judge will hear the brief but necessary testimony that legal reasons exist to grant a divorce. Thereafter, the judge will review and sign the Judgment of Divorce. At this point, your divorce is final.

It is suggested that, prior to this finalization, each of you buy an hour or two of an attorney's time and have the proposed Judgment of Divorce reviewed. It is helpful to work with lawyers who understand mediation and the originality that often comes with mediation. Usually mediators have a list of attorneys who are familiar with the process and who have the necessary creativity. The purpose of this review is to ensure that you have made well-informed and wise decisions. Hence, when your divorce is completed, you can feel secure and assured that you have been conscientious and responsible as you divided your assets and established your parenting plan.

Now let's check back on Tricia and Tom. Although they have done marital counseling and decided to exercise forgiveness and to rebuild their marriage on the five components, things have not gone well. Accordingly, they set up a four-month working separation. At the time of reassessment, they decided to pursue a divorce.

At this point, they are able to leave the marriage with more understanding of their respective contributions to the marital breakdown and with less blame. They have exercised forgiveness of themselves, each other, and Tom for his affair. And they have decided to complete the divorce via the divorce mediation process.

Early in the mediation process, the mediators encourage them to clarify their ideals for their lives post-divorce regarding their relationship with one another, the co-parenting of their children, and the division of their assets. Their shared lists looks as follows.

Tricia and Tom's Ideals for Their
Post-Divorce Relationship

1. Remain congenial enough to talk regularly about the children, make joint decisions, and attend their school conferences and functions simultaneously.
2. Continue contact with each other's extended family, but do so when the ex-spouse is not present.
3. Encourage friends to continue their relationship with both of us, but invite us over separately and not discuss our ex-spouse with us.
4. Give each other privacy and distance as we re-establish our personal lives.

Tricia and Tom's Ideals for Their
Post-Divorce Co-Parenting

1. Support each other with the children.
2. Encourage easy and frequent contact with the other parent.
3. Have regular phone conversations with each other, perhaps at a designated time, to discuss parenting issues and decisions.
4. Keep the family home and have Tricia and the children remain in the house so that this, along with peer relationships, school, and school involvement, can remain constant for the children.
5. Have Tom live within the same school district so that the children can have easy access to him as well as continuity in their friendships and school life.
6. Have shared parenting, so that Tom will have the children while Tricia is in Washington, D.C., each month.
7. When either will be gone for a significant length of time, give the other the opportunity to be with the children before making alternate arrangements.
8. Be flexible with each other about holiday and vacation time with the children.
9. Allow each other to teach his or her respective values.

10. Encourage the children's relationships with the ex-spouse's extended family.
11. Advise each other of special activities and achievements related to the children.
12. Respect the children's increased outside involvements and work with their schedules.
13. Make joint provision for the children's college education.

Tricia and Tom's Ideals for Their Post-Divorce Division of Assets

1. Each take his or her own family heirlooms, gifts, and personal belongings.
2. Divide the household goods in a fair, equitable, and practical manner.
3. Keep his or her respective retirement funds. (It should be noted that Tricia and Tom are in a unique situation. More commonly, the husband has either the only or the larger retirement fund. Often, spouses decide to divide this in such a way that the wife as well as the husband has a nest egg for the future.)
4. Since the children will continue to live in the house to allow for continuity in their lives during this time of change, ensure that Tricia's income meets the expenses.
5. Divide and rearrange assets so there is enough liquidity for Tom to purchase a home in the same neighborhood and school district.
6. Make a financial plan for the children's college education. (It should be noted that in most states this is not required by law. One of the advantages of mediation is that couples can tailor their divorce to their specific needs and desires.)
7. Each keep his or her own vehicle.
8. Divide the assets in a fair and equitable manner.

With these ideals or shared goals in mind, mediation can begin. After discussion and consideration of various options about co-parenting and division of assets, Tricia and Tom can reach win/win agreements. For illustrative purposes, a Memorandum of Agreement and Judgment of Divorce are included. These serve to demonstrate the type of agreements that are jointly and amicably made. Although divorce is painful, divorce mediation allows partners to make the best of a difficult situation. They can plan responsibly for their own and their children's futures.

MEMORANDUM OF AGREEMENT

Patricia L. Sinclair and Thomas J. Sinclair have agreed to submit the issues of their divorce to the mediation process and have retained as their mediators attorney James B. Howard and psychologist Dr. Linda Hertel Dykstra.

Tricia and Tom have agreed that both have made a full disclosure of the identity and value of all of their assets and liabilities. They have endeavored, through the process of mediation, to achieve fair and reasonable agreements, and both feel they have achieved a settlement which is fair to each of them.

The parties now desire to set forth the agreement which they have reached during the mediation process, and it is their desire that this Memorandum of Agreement be taken to their respective attorneys so those attorneys can review and implement their agreement by obtaining from them a dissolution of their marriage based upon this settlement. The parties understand that if either wishes to seek modification of the provisions of the Memorandum of Agreement by virtue of recommendations of their respective attorneys, they can return to the mediators to resolve such requests for modification.

Tom and Tricia have accepted the mediation process as a dignified and reasonable technique for resolving differences, and they understand that, if a dispute arises between them in the future, they can avail themselves of the mediation process in order to resolve any such disputes.

Tom and Tricia have agreed as follows:

Personal Relationship

Tom and Tricia have agreed that, although they are going to go forward with their divorce, they wish their future relationship to remain congenial enough to be able to talk regularly about their children, make joint decisions regarding them, and attend their children's school conferences and functions simultaneously.

They both will support continued contact with each other's extended family but agree that this contact will occur when the ex-spouse is not present.

Tom and Tricia will encourage friends to continue friendships with both of them. However, they will also advise their friends to invite them to separate functions and not discuss matters concerning the ex-spouse.

Tom and Tricia are committed to respect each other's privacy so each can reestablish his or her personal life.

Co-Parenting

Tom and Tricia agree to support each other in parenting the children and will not undermine each other. They will encourage the children to have easy and frequent contact with the other parent. They also agree that both parents will teach the children their respective values. Tom and Tricia agree to respect the children's increased outside involvements and are willing to work with the children's schedules.

They agree that regular communication is important to co-parenting the children and are committed that on each Wednesday night, between 9:00 and 10:00 p.m., Tom will call Tricia to discuss parenting issues and decisions. At this time, they will also advise one another of special activities and achievements related to the children.

Custody and Visitation

Tom and Tricia have agreed to joint physical and legal custody. This means they will share the custody of the children on an alternating basis, and they will share in the making of important decisions that relate to the children.

The children will live primarily with Tricia. However, since Tricia travels out of the state at least one week each month, Tom will have the children during that week beginning after school at 4:00 p.m. on Thursday, through the next week until the following Monday, when he will return the children to school. In order to facilitate this custodial arrangement, Tom has agreed that Tricia will continue to reside with the children in the marital home, and he will purchase a home in the same school district.

In addition to the above-described custodial arrangement, Tom and Tricia have agreed as follows:

a. Tom will have visitation every Thursday evening from 4:00 p.m. until 8:00 p.m.

b. Tricia and Tom will alternate visitation on the children's spring break. In addition, both Tricia and Tom will have visitation for at least one week of the children's two-week Christmas vacation on an alternating basis.

c. Tricia and Tom will alternate visitation with the children on the following holidays: Memorial Day, Fourth of July, Labor Day, Thanksgiving, Christmas Eve, Christmas Day, and Easter.

d. Tricia will have visitation with the children every Mother's Day, and Tom will have visitation with the children every Father's Day.

e. Tricia and Tom intend to celebrate the children's birthdays separately within their usual custody/visitation schedule.

f. Tricia and Tom will have reasonable and liberal visitation with the children at such other times upon which they mutually agree.

Whenever Tom or Tricia is out of town, they agree to give the other parent the opportunity to be with the children before making other arrangements for the children's care.

Child Support*

Tom has agreed to pay the sum of $250.00 per week in child support for the care of Matthew and Stephanie. The $250.00 per week in child support will be reduced to $150.00 per week when Matthew reaches the age of eighteen or graduates from high school, whichever is later. The $150.00 per week in child support shall continue until Stephanie reaches the age of eighteen or graduates from high school, whichever is later.

Taxes

Tom and Tricia have agreed that Tricia will be permitted to claim the children as an income tax deduction on her federal, state, and city income tax returns. Tricia will be permitted to claim those deductions for as long as the parties have shared physical custody of the children.

College Fund**

Tricia and Tom agree that their children should receive a college education. They each agree to contribute $2,500.00 on or before April 15 of each year commencing April 15, 2000. They will continue to make contributions to the account until both children

---

*Child support payments are calculated via the Michigan Child Support Manual, which takes into consideration both the amount of time both spouses parent the children and their respective incomes.

**This is a unique provision that Tricia and Tom wished to incorporate into their agreement. It is not required by Michigan law. Divorce mediation allows each couple to tailor an agreement to their specific wishes and needs.

have graduated from college or the children have expressed their intent not to obtain a college education.

Alimony***

Tom and Tricia have discussed the issue of alimony and have decided that, in light of their respective incomes, neither party will receive any alimony.

Health Care Expenses

Tricia will continue to maintain all health care insurance as is available through her employers, Van, Lee, & Smith, for the benefit of the children.

Tricia and Tom will pay any deductibles and uninsured medical, dental, orthodontal, ophthamological, and psychological expenses relating to the children on a 50/50 basis.

Life Insurance

Both Tom and Tricia will maintain the children as beneficiaries of a life insurance policy on their respective lives in the amount of $100,000 for as long as the children are minors.

Pension

Tom and Tricia recognize that the law provides that they may each have an interest in each other's pensions. However, since the pensions are relatively equal, they have agreed that each may keep his or her pension, free of any interest by the other party.

***Alimony is generally applicable only to marriages of long duration, usually 15 years or more, and/or when other significant criteria specified are met.

Property Division

Tom and Tricia have agreed that Tricia will receive the marital home, located at 14100 Ruby Lane, Rochester Hills, Michigan, and legally described as:

> Lot 4 of T and S Plat, an addition to the City of
> Rochester Hills, Section 23, Town 6 North, Range 12
> West, Rochester Hills, Michigan, according to the
> recorded plat thereof.

Tricia will pay to Tom the sum of $50,000, which represents one half of the equity in the home at the present time. Tom will use these funds to purchase a home in the children's school district. Tom will execute a Quit Claim Deed conveying his interest in the above-described property to Tricia. Thereafter, Tricia will be solely responsible for paying any mortgages, debts, or taxes relating to the above property and she will hold Tom harmless.

Tricia will receive her 2000 Mazda Miata. Tom will receive his 1999 Ford Ranger.

Tricia and Tom will receive their personal effects and family heirlooms.

Tricia and Tom will divide on an alternating selection basis all family pictures and household furnishings.

Debts

Tom and Tricia will pay any debts incurred in their own name since the filing of the Complaint for Divorce.

THE ABOVE FULLY AND COMPLETELY SETS FORTH
THE AGREEMENT OF THE PARTIES REACHED THROUGH
THE MEDIATION PROCESS. BOTH ACKNOWLEDGE THAT
BY SIGNING THIS AGREEMENT THEY ARE VOLUNTARILY
ENTERING INTO THIS AGREEMENT AND PROMISE TO
ABIDE BY ITS TERMS. FURTHER, THEY ACKNOWLEDGE
THAT THERE ARE NO OTHER AGREEMENTS REACHED
BETWEEN THE PARTIES THAT ARE NOT SET FORTH
HEREIN.

Dated: _____, 20__   _____
                                                Patricia L. Sinclair

Dated: _____, 20__   _____
                                                Thomas J. Sinclair

    This concludes the Memorandum of Agreement. The formal
Judgment of Divorce follows. It legally completes the divorce
process. Please note the difference in language and format between
the Memorandum of Agreement and the Judgment of Divorce.

JUDGMENT OF DIVORCE

STATE OF MICHIGAN
IN THE CIRCUIT COURT FOR THE COUNTY OF OAKLAND

PATRICIA L. SINCLAIR,

    Plaintiff,   File No. 93-10206-DM

v   *JUDGMENT OF DIVORCE*

THOMAS J. SINCLAIR,

    Defendant.

_____/

    At a session of said Court held in the Circuit Court
for the County of Oakland, Rochester Hills, Michigan
on this _____ day of _____, 20____.
PRESENT: *The Honorable George W. Bushki*
                Circuit Court Judge

THIS MATTER having come on to be heard upon the Plaintiff's Complaint for Divorce filed herein, taken as confessed by the Defendant, his Stipulation to Proceed having been entered of record, and the Plaintiff having presented evidence in open Court from which the Court finds that there has been a breakdown in the marriage relationship to the extent that the objects of matrimony have been destroyed and there remains no reasonable likelihood that the marriage can be preserved and that the Plaintiff is entitled to a Judgment of Divorce;

NOW THEREFORE, IT IS HEREBY ORDERED:

Divorce

The bonds of matrimony between Patricia L. Sinclair and Thomas J. Sinclair are hereby dissolved pursuant to the Michigan Statutes Annotated, Section 25.86 (3).

Custody

Pursuant to MCL 722.226(a), the Plaintiff and the Defendant shall have the joint physical care, custody and control of their minor children, Matthew Sinclair, born March 20, 1990, and Stephanie Sinclair, born August 22, 1993, until said children attain the age of eighteen (18) or graduate from high school, whichever is later, or until further order of the Court. It is specifically understood by the parties that joint physical custody means that Matthew Sinclair and Stephanie Sinclair shall reside alternately for specified periods of time with both the Plaintiff and the Defendant.

The parties shall conduct themselves at all times with the best interests of the minor children foremost in their consideration, and they shall communicate with each other on a regular basis to share in the making of important decisions that relate to the children, so as to enhance and foster such best interests of the children.

The Defendant shall call the Plaintiff on each and every Wednesday evening between the hours of 9:00 and 10:00 p.m. to discuss and decide all important decisions relating to the children.

Inherent Rights of the Minor Children

The minor children of the parties have the inherent right to the natural affections and love of both parents, and neither party shall do anything which may estrange the minor children from the other party or attempt to discredit or cause disrespect or diminish the natural affections of the minor children for the other party.

Waiver of Home Investigation

The home investigation by the Friend of the Court is hereby waived.

Visitation

Since the Plaintiff and Defendant have been awarded the joint physical custody of their minor children, the children shall alternately reside with each parent on the following schedule:

a. The children shall reside with the Plaintiff except for those times set forth below when they shall reside with the Defendant.

b. For at least one week per month, the Defendant shall have the children commencing on Thursday at 4:00 p.m. through the following week and ending on Monday morning when the Defendant shall return the children to school. In addition, the Defendant shall have visitation on every Thursday evening from 4:00 p.m. until 8:00 p.m.

c. The Plaintiff and Defendant shall alternate visitation on the children's spring break. In addition, both the Plaintiff and the Defendant shall have visitation for at least one week of the children's two-week Christmas vacation on an alternating basis.

d. The parties shall alternate visitation with the minor children on the following holidays: Memorial Day, Fourth of July, Labor Day, Thanksgiving, Christmas Eve, Christmas Day, and Easter.

e. The Plaintiff shall have visitation with the parties' minor children on every Mother's Day and the Defendant shall have visitation with the parties' minor children on every Father's Day.

f. The Plaintiff and Defendant intend to celebrate the children's birthdays separately within their usual custody/visitation schedule.

g. Both the Plaintiff and the Defendant shall have reasonable and liberal visitation with the parties' minor children at such other times upon which they mutually agree.

Child Support

The Defendant, Thomas J. Sinclair, shall pay to the office of the Oakland County Friend of the Court the sum of $250.00 per week for the support and maintenance of the parties' minor children, Matthew Sinclair, born March 20, 1990, and Stephanie Sinclair, born August 22, 1993, commencing the first Monday following the entry of the Judgment of Divorce. The sum of $250.00 per week in child support shall be allocated between the children as follows: $100.00 for Matthew Sinclair and $150.00 for Stephanie Sinclair.

Said child support shall be paid until each child attains the age of eighteen (18) years or graduates from high school, whichever is later, if the child is regularly attending high school on a full-time basis with a reasonable expectation of completing sufficient credits to graduate from high school while residing on a full-time basis with the payee of support but in no case after the child reaches nineteen (19) years and six (6) months of age or until further order of the Court.

Retroactive Modification

Except as provided in Section 3 of the Support and Visitation Enforcement Act, Act Number 295 of the Public Acts of 1982, being Section 552.603 of the Michigan Compiled Laws, a support order that is a part of a Judgment or is an order in a domestic relations matter as that term is defined in Section 31 of the Friend of the Court Act, Act Number 294 of the Public Acts of 1982, being Section 552.531 of the Michigan Compiled Laws, is a Judgment on or after the date each support payment is due, with full force, effect, and attributes of a Judgment of this state and is not on or after the date it is due subject to retroactive modifications.

Supervisory Fee

The payer of child support shall pay to the office of the Oakland County Friend of the Court as a supervisory fee the sum of $3.25 each month for so long as support shall be ordered in this cause.

Order of Income Withholding

Child support ordered herein shall be subject to an immediate Order of Income Withholding, pursuant to Public Act 296 of 1990. The Oakland County Friend of the Court is hereby directed to provide the payer's source of income with the appropriate notice and order necessary to implement this order and the requirements of Public Act 296 of 1990.

Name and Address of the Payer's Employer

The payer of child support shall immediately notify in writing the Oakland County Friend of the Court of the name and address of any subsequent employer. The Plaintiff is presently employed by Van, Lee, & Smith at 555 Peninsular Center, Detroit, Michigan. The Defendant is presently a self-employed veterinarian, at 1034 Chester, SE, Rochester Hills, Michigan.

Taxes

The Plaintiff and Defendant have agreed that Plaintiff will be permitted to claim the children as an income tax deduction on her federal, state, and city income tax returns. Plaintiff will be permitted to claim those deductions for as long as the parties have shared physical custody of the children.

Health Care Insurance

The Plaintiff, Patricia L. Sinclair, shall continue to maintain all health care insurance as is available through her employer, Van, Lee, & Smith for the benefit of the minor children.

The parties shall pay any deductibles and uninsured medical, dental, orthodontic, ophthalmologic, and psychological expenses relating to the minor children on a 50/50 basis.

The parties are required to fully cooperate in exchanging material and information necessary to utilize health care insurance and accomplish the payment of unreimbursed expenses.

The parties shall notify the Oakland County Friend of the Court of any health care coverage that is available to them as a benefit of employment or that is maintained by them; the name of the insurance company, the health care organization, or health maintenance organization; the policy, certificate or contract number; and the names and birth dates of the persons for whose benefit they maintain health care coverage under the policy, certificate, or contract.

Consolidated Omnibus Reconciliation Act
of 1985 *(C.O.B.R.A.)*

The Defendant shall provide notice to the Plaintiff's employer, Van, Lee, & Smith, pursuant to the Consolidated Omnibus Reconciliation Act of 1985, that he is entitled, at his election, to a continuation of health insurance under the employer's health insurance plan. The Defendant shall be responsible for the cost of any future coverage provided under the plan.

Address and Domicile of the Minor Children

Neither the domicile nor residence of the minor children shall be removed from the State of Michigan without prior approval of the Court.

The parties shall notify, in writing, the Oakland County Friend of the Court of any subsequent change of address while any provisions of this Judgment are in full force and effect. The Plaintiff's current address is 14100 Ruby Lane, Rochester Hills, Michigan. The Defendant's current address is 11842 Linden Circle, Rochester Hills, Michigan.

Life Insurance

The Plaintiff and the Defendant shall maintain the children as beneficiaries of a life insurance policy on their respective lives in the amount of $100,000 for so long as the children are minors.

Alimony

Neither the Plaintiff nor the Defendant shall be awarded alimony, nor is alimony reserved to either party.

Property Settlement

The Plaintiff shall receive, free and clear of any claims by the Defendant, the marital home at 14100 Ruby Lane, Rochester Hills, Michigan, and legally described as:

> Lot 4 of P and S Plat, an addition to the City of
> Rochester Hills, Section 23, Town 6 North, Range
> 12 West, Rochester Hills, Michigan, according to
> the recorded plat thereof.

The Plaintiff shall forthwith pay to the Defendant the sum of $50,000 as compensation for Defendant's interest in the marital home. Thereafter, the Defendant shall forthwith execute a Quit Claim Deed conveying his interest in the above described property to the Plaintiff. Thereafter, the Plaintiff shall be solely responsible for paying any mortgages, debts, or taxes relating to the above property and she shall hold the Defendant harmless thereon.

The Plaintiff shall receive as her sole and separate property, free of any claims by the Defendant, her 2000 Mazda Miata. The

Defendant shall receive as his sole and separate property, free of any claims by the Plaintiff, his 1999 Ford Ranger.

The Plaintiff and the Defendant shall have as their sole and separate property, free and clear of any claims by the other party, their personal effects and family heirlooms.

The Plaintiff and the Defendant shall divide on an alternating selection basis all family pictures and household furnishings.

Debts

The Plaintiff and Defendant shall be responsible for paying any debts incurred in their own name since the filing of the Complaint of Divorce.

College Expense

Commencing April 15, 2000, and each and every April 15 thereafter, the Plaintiff and Defendant shall contribute the sum of $2,500 each to their children's college fund. Thereafter, they shall agree between themselves as to how those funds should be expended for the benefit of their children's college expenses. College contributions as required herein shall continue until both children have graduated from college, unless the parties agree otherwise.

Pension, Annuity, Or Retirement Benefits

Both the Plaintiff and Defendant shall be entitled to receive, free and clear of any interest of the other party, their known pension, annuity, or retirement benefits which they have accrued as a result of their respective employment, including their known contributions to such pension, annuity, or retirement benefits, and their rights or contingent rights in and to unvested pension, annuity, or retirement benefits.

Statutory Insurance

Any rights of either party to any policy or contract of life, endowment, or annuity insurance of the other as beneficiary are hereby extinguished unless specifically preserved by this Judgment.

Dower

The provisions made in the Judgment of Divorce shall be in lieu of the dower rights of each party in the property of the other, and shall be in full satisfaction of all claims which each may have in any property the other now owns or which the other has an interest, or in which the other may hereafter own or have an interest.

Execution of Documents

The parties hereto shall execute, acknowledge, and deliver to each other, as and when required, any and all deeds, assignments, insurance applications, or other instruments of release, assurance, or transfer or conveyance required to effectuate the terms and provisions hereof; provided in the event that either of the said parties shall fail, refuse, or neglect to execute, acknowledge, and deliver and instrument required to implement the terms and provisions of the Judgment of Divorce, then said Judgment shall be self-executing and shall stand in the place and stead of any of the instruments required hereunder; further, a certified copy of this Judgment of Divorce may be recorded in the office of any Register of Deeds, Secretary of State, or other public office hereto to have the same force and effect as if said instrument had in fact been executed.

Retention of Jurisdiction

This Court shall retain jurisdiction of this cause and over the parties hereto for the purpose of assuring compliance with the provisions of this Judgment of Divorce.

This Court reserves the right to make such other and further Orders which it shall deem necessary to implement this Judgment which are not otherwise inconsistent with the terms hereof.

Disclosure By The Parties

Each of the parties hereto has made a full and complete disclosure to the other party of all assets acquired during the course of the parties' marriage, and the Judgment contains a complete itemization of the aforesaid assets and the agreement upon distribution thereof.

WHEN THE JUDGMENT BECOMES FINAL

This Judgment of Divorce shall be given effect immediately and forthwith upon entry hereof.

———————————————————
Circuit Court Judge

EXAMINED, COUNTERSIGNED   ATTEST: A TRUE COPY
AND ENTERED BY ME:

———————————————   ———————————————
Deputy Clerk   Deputy Clerk

The within parties and their attorneys agree that the terms of this Judgment of Divorce accurately reflect the agreement which they have made, and they further agree that notice of entry of this Judgment of Divorce may be waived and approve this form for entry:

———————————————   ———————————————
Patricia L. Sinclair   Thomas J. Sinclair
Plaintiff   Defendant

———————————————   ———————————————
Attorney for Plaintiff   Attorney for Defendant

As noted earlier, this Judgment of Divorce should be reviewed by outside lawyers to ensure that Tricia and Tom's best interests have been safeguarded. If there are any suggestions, Tom and Tricia can return to mediation to discuss them. If there are none, they move forward with the legal process. On the appointed day, Tricia, who is the plaintiff, and her attorney will go to court. After Tricia answers a few standard questions on the stand, the judge will sign the Judgment of Divorce, and the divorce process will be complete.

It is sad when a marriage ends. However, to dissolve it via divorce mediation is the more humane method. Tricia and Tom were empowered. They maintained control of the process. With the assistance of the mediators, they constructively shared their goals and feelings and then made the necessary decisions in a well-informed manner. Further, with mediation, they were able to retain the insight and growth gained in therapy as well as keep the best interests of their children foremost at all times.

Couples are able to end their marriage responsibly. They can thoughtfully plan for both their own and their children's futures. Parenting needs to continue in as consistent and supportive a manner as possible. Even though the marriage ends, parenting does not. Mediation facilitates continued cooperation in this dimension.

If divorce is inevitable, mediation allows you to take charge of the process. You become educated and empowered to make your own decisions. Through divorce mediation, you can make agreements that are win/win and can be honored in a spirit of cooperation. If parenting arrangements need to be altered, you can either mediate between yourselves or return to the formal process and use mediators. When you do your divorce via the mediation process, it allows you to be mutually supportive to your children and each other now and throughout the years to come.

REBUILDING

CHAPTER 11

TASKS OF ADJUSTMENT

W hen a relationship ends, it is essential to move through the post-divorce adjustment process. This is a period of major shift and change. The greater the understanding and closure you gain, the more prepared you are to fully enter your future. The more emotionally finished and at peace you are, the better for you and your children.

In order to close this chapter of your life and begin the next, it is important to complete the tasks of adjustment. You must (1) understand why the marriage ended, (2) experience the related grief, (3) learn to be single, (4) refocus on the five major components, (5) move forward and, if desired, invest in a new relationship.

UNDERSTAND THE MARITAL BREAKDOWN

Tricia and Tom were conscientious about diagnosis and resolution of the trouble spots in their relationship. They worked diligently on the issue of forgiveness. Eventually, they divorced via divorce mediation. They had a thorough understanding of why their marriage ended.

If your relationship is over, it is critical for you too to understand why your marriage broke down. Perhaps this book has helped you clarify where your non-negotiable values were mismatched and on which of the other dimensions–empathy, assertiveness, unconditional love, or compromise–you and your mate functioned poorly. Now you can appreciate why safety and vulnerability were minimal, and why emotional and sexual intimacy were marginal. If there was an affair, you can understand why it occurred. You can evaluate whether the process of forgiveness was completed. If you divorced via the traditional legal method, you can see how conflict between you and your partner may have intensified during the divorce process.

It is important to be clear about why your marriage dissolved, not only for your own but also for your children's sake. When they ask why you divorced, you need to know so you are able to explain to them, as you deem appropriate, both the reasons for the divorce and the responsibility that both of you bear. To blame your partner is not helpful to anyone. It leaves you with bitterness and your children with an even deeper sense of pain and loss. Your children need to be free to love both of you.

GRIEVE

It is essential not only to appreciate why the marriage ended but also to come to grips with the full emotional impact of the divorce. Your dream of a life-long marriage and intact family is gone. Even when you understand why it ended, it is still a significant loss. Accordingly, it is critical to feel the grief.

Often, the official date of the divorce is unrelated to the completion of grief. If you were able to foresee the demise of your marriage, you may have done what is called anticipatory grieving. You began to experience sorrow before the actual divorce. However, if it came rather suddenly, you may need to complete the grief process long after the divorce has been finalized.

Whether you ultimately finish your grieving in advance of the divorce or long after it is finalized, it needs to be done. If you get stuck, you may wish to seek professional assistance. The goal is to grieve and heal so that you can move forward.

Tom and Tricia need to go through this same process. After they divorce, they initially may feel a sense of relief. However, although each has done some anticipatory grieving, they still need to complete the process, post-divorce. When they met in Florida, they had great dreams for their relationship. Their expectations did not and will not materialize. They are no longer a couple. The two-parent intact family they wished to provide for their children is gone. They grieve the loss of their dreams.

RELEARN SINGLENESS

In addition to knowing the reasons for the marital breakdown and finishing the grief process, it is important to learn to live as a single person. You will need to parent alone, manage the finances, get the car repaired, shop, cook, entertain, make new friends, and travel independently or with other single people.

Tricia and Tom also will need to go through the experience of being single. Since they lived fairly independently while under the same roof, they have a start on this task. However, now they each need to entertain as a solo person, be a single parent, and carry the entire responsibility for the household alone.

It should be noted that, in contrast to Tricia's experience, many women in this society have not lived on their own. It is not uncommon for a woman to move from her father's house to her husband's home. Without living independently, she does not learn how to be self-sufficient and have a strong sense of self.

When divorce occurs, she gets a second chance to be single and complete the developmental task related to self-sufficiency. It is important to take this opportunity and make the most of it.

Being single and learning to be whole and complete in and of yourself is a challenge that many people, both male and female, wish to avoid. They prefer to get into a new relationship immediately and become part of a couple. Just a word of caution: a relationship started before or soon after a divorce often does not last long. It falters and often fails because considerable insight and growth are afoot. The tasks of adjustment result in change. Therefore, if you are divorcing or recently divorced, give yourself a minimum of one year to complete the adjustment process before you enter a serious relationship.

REFOCUS

During this time of intense and sometimes painful learning and growth, it is important to redefine your non-negotiable values and fine-tune your ability to practice empathy, assertiveness, unconditional love, and compromise. After doing this, you are prepared to choose friends and, if desired, a partner with whom you can design a relationship which incorporates the five critical components.

Although Tricia and Tom have refocused during therapy, they must continue post-divorce. Then they too will be in a position to choose new friends and possibly a future mate.

BEGIN AGAIN

In all likelihood, the person you will choose after completion of the adjustment process will be different from the person you would have selected before or during. If you marry before the tasks are finished, your incomplete learning and unresolved emotions will impact the next relationship. Cutting short the process may be part of the reason why second marriages all too frequently end in divorce.

The diagram that follows summarizes the adjustment process.

Adjustment Process

FIRST MARRIAGE	MINIMUM OF ONE YEAR	SECOND MARRIAGE
DIVORCE	1. Understand why the marriage ended. 2. Grieve the loss of the marriage and of the corresponding dreams. 3. Learn to be single and self-sufficient. 4. Refocus. Clarify your non-negotiable values and practice empathy, assertiveness, unconditional love, and compromise. 5. Begin again. Use these five components as your criteria as you date and possibly select a mate.	

When the adjustment process is complete and a subsequent marriage is designed and built on the five components, that marriage can endure over time. In this relationship, it will be safe to be vulnerable. Emotional and sexual intimacy can thrive. Daily forgiveness will comfortably occur.

As Betsy and Ben demonstrate, a relationship can be extremely fulfilling. Being married to your best friend is one of the greatest joys in life.

AFTERWORD

At this point, we have come full circle. We conclude this study of relationships where we began, with the focus on the five dimensions for an enduring relationship. Whether you are in a position to select a mate, restructure your present relationship, divorce, or begin again, it is my hope that this book has been of assistance. Best wishes as you move forward with life and love.

FOR FURTHER READING

1. VALUES

Baier, Kurt, and Nicholas Rescher, eds. *Values and the Future*. New York: The Free Press, 1969.

Carkhuff, Robert R. *The Art of Problem-Solving*. Amherst, Massachusetts: Human Resource Development Press, 1973.

Eisenberg, Nancy, Janusz, Reykowski, and Ervin Staub, eds. *Social and Moral Values: Individual and Societal Perspectives*. Hillsdale, New Jersey: Lawrence Erlbaum Associates, Publishers, 1989.

Hart, Gordon M., Ph.D. *Values Clarification for Counselors*. Springfield, Illinois: Charles C. Thomas, Publisher, 1978.

Peterson, James Allan. *Counseling and Values*. Scranton, Pennsylvania: International Text Book Company, 1970.

Schnael, Maxine. *Limits: A Search for New Values*. New York: Clarkson and Potter, Inc., Publishers, 1981.

Simon, Sidney B., Leland W. Howe, and Howard Kirschenbaum. *Values Clarification: A Handbook of Practical Strategies for Teachers and Students.* New York: Hart Publishing Company, Inc., 1972.

2.   ASSERTIVENESS

Alberti, Robert E., Ph.D., and Michael L. Emmons, Ph.D. *Stand Up, Speak Out, Talk Back! The Key to Self-Assertive Behavior.* New York: Pocket Books, 1970.

Butler, Pamela E. *Self-Assertiveness for Women.* San Francisco: Harper and Row, Publishers, 1981.

Fensterheim, Herbert, Ph.D., and Jean Baer. *Don't Say Yes When You Want to Say No.* New York: Dell Publishing Company, Inc., 1975.

Palmer, Pat, Ed.D. *The Mouse, the Monster and Me.* San Luis Obispo, California: Impact Publishers, 1984.

Smith, Manuel J., Ph.D. *When I Say No, I Feel Guilty.* New York: Bantam Books, 1975.

Bloom, Lynn Z., Karen Coburn, and Joan Pearlman. *The New Assertive Woman.* New York: Delacorte Press, 1975.

3.   DYSFUNCTIONAL FAMILY

Bass, Ellen and Laura Davis. *The Courage to Heal.* New York: Harper and Row, 1988.

Bass, Ellen and Laura Davis. *The Courage to Heal Workbook.* New York: Harper and Row, 1990.

Beattie, Melody. *Codependent No More.* New York: Harper and Row,1987.

Blume, E. Sue. *Secret Survivors: Uncovering Incest and Its Aftereffects in Women.* New York: Ballantine Books, 1990.

Bradshaw, John. *Healing the Shame That Binds You.* Deerfield Beach, Florida: Health Communications, Inc., 1988.

Clark, Jean I. *Growing Up Again; How to Parent Yourself So You Can Parent Your Children.* San Francisco, California: Harper and Row, 1989.

Covington, Stephanie, and Liana Becket. *Leaving the Enchanted Forest: The Path from Relationship Addiction to Intimacy.* San Francisco: Harper and Row, 1988.

Forward, Susan, M.S., and Craig Buck. *Betrayal of Innocence.* Harmondsworth, Middlesex, England: Penguin Books, Ltd., 1978.

Forward, Susan. *Toxic Parents: Overcoming Their Hurtful Legacy and Reclaiming Your Life.* New York: Bantam Books, 1989.

Friel, John, Ph.D., and Linda Friel, M.A. *An Adult Child's Guide to What's "Normal."* Deerfield Beach, Florida: Health Communications, Inc., 1990.

Graber, Ken. *Ghost in the Bedroom: A Guide for Partners of Incest Survivors.* Deerfield Beach, Florida: Health Communications, Inc., 1991.

McCabe, Thomas R., Ph.D. *Victims No More.* Center City, Minnesota: Hazelden, 1978.

Norwood, Robin. *Women Who Love Too Much.* Los Angeles: Jeremy P. Tarcher, Inc., 1985.

Wegscheider, Sharon. *Another Chance: Hope and Health for the Alcoholic Family.* Palo Alto, California: Science and Behavior Books, Inc., 1981.

4. FORGIVENESS

Augsburger, David. *Caring Enough to Forgive: True Forgiveness.* Scottsdale, Pennsylvania: Herald Press, 1981.

Augsburger, David. *The Freedom of Forgiveness, 70 x 7.* Chicago: Moody Press, 1970.

Carder, Dave. *Torn Asunder: Recovering From Extramarital Affairs.* Chicago: Moody Press, 1992.

Hosier, Helen. *It Feels Good to Forgive.* Irvine, California: Harvest House Publishers, 1974.

Smedes, Lewis B. *Forgive and Forget: Healing the Hurts We Don't Deserve.* New York: Pocket Books, 1984.

Walters, Richard P. *Forgive and Be Free: Healing the Wounds of Past And Present.* Grand Rapids, Michigan: Zondervan, 1983.

5. MEDIATION

Ahrons, Constance R. *The Good Divorce: Keeping Your Family Together When Your Marriage Comes Apart.* New York: Harper Collins Publishers, 1994.

Fisher, Roger, and Scott Brown. *Getting Together: Building a Relationship That Gets to Yes.* Boston: Houghton Mifflin Company, 1988.

Fisher, Roger, and William Ury. *Getting to Yes.* New York: Penguin Books, 1981.

Folberg, Jay and Alison Taylor. *Mediation: A Comprehensive Guide to Resolving Conflict Without Litigation.* San Francisco, California: Jossey-Bass, Inc., 1984.

Gardner, Richard A., M.D. *The Parent's Book About Divorce.* New York: Bantam Books, 1977.

Irving, Howard H. *Divorce Mediation: A Rational Alternative to the Adversary System.* New York: Universe Books, 1981.

Kahn, Lynn Sandra, Ph.D. *Peacemaking: A Systems Approach to Conflict Management.* Lanham, Maryland: University Press of America, 1988.

6. GRIEF/DIVORCE/CHILDREN AND DIVORCE

Fisher, Bruce. *Rebuilding When Your Relationship Ends.* San Luis Obispo, California: Impact Publishers, 1981.

Galper, Miriam. *Joint Custody and Co-Parenting.* Baltimore, Maryland: Port City Press, 1981.

Heimlinger, Trudy. *After You've Said Goodbye.* Sacramento, California: Brooks Publishing Company, 1982.

Krantzler, Mel. *Creative Divorce.* New York: Signet, 1973.

Ricci, Isolina, Ph.D. *Mom's House, Dad's House.* New York: Collier Books, 1980.

Smoke, Jim. *Growing Through Divorce.* Eugene, Oregon: Harvest House Publishers, 1983.

Triere, Lynette and Richard Peacock. *Learning to Leave: A Woman's Guide.* Chicago, Illinois: Contemporary Books, Inc., 1982.

Westberg, Granger E. *Good Grief.* Philadelphia: Fortress Press, 1971.

Additional copies of this book may be ordered from:

Mediation Center of Grand Rapids
2716 East Paris S.E.
Grand Rapids, Michigan 49546